Instructor's Resource Manual to Accompany

Public Speaking in a Diverse Society

by Patricia Kearney and Timothy G. Plax

California State University at Long Beach

Sidonie Squier
Patricia Kearney
Timothy G. Plax

Mayfield Publishing Company
Mountain View, California
London • Toronto

International Standard Book Number: 1-55934-289-7

Manufactured in the United States of America
10 9 8 7 6 5 4 3 2 1

Mayfield Publishing Company
1280 Villa Street
Mountain View, California 94041

CONTENTS

ACKNOWLEDGMENTS

The authors want to give formal recognition to the following faculty and teaching associates for their insightful comments, helpful suggestions, and assistance in piloting both the materials contained in this manual and *Public Speaking in a Diverse Society:* Dr. Sharon Downey, Dr. Nancy Burroughs-Denhart, Rosemary Swade, Analisa Ridenour, Steve Mortensen, Jenny Graber, Rick Kung, Jim Bonstein, John Lervold, Jennifer Waldeck, Victoria Orrego, Leslie Zimmerman, Carolyn Shepard, Sandy Kalander, Felyce Thomas, Andrea Amper, Angela McCaskill, Robin Derr Matthews, Vandye Forrester, Debby McPherson, Carol Bertolero, and Steve Arthur. Thank you!

INTRODUCTION

An introductory public speaking course can be organized in a variety of ways, and the material in the text can be used in different ways by different teachers. As the teacher, you must decide how much emphasis to give each chapter and how early or late a particular chapter should be read by your students. Moreover, you will need to decide how to balance theory and principles with actual classroom practice in skills. You will need to determine how much time to devote to lectures, class discussions, activities, speeches, and other assignments. These decisions will be based on the number of students enrolled in your course, the number of class meetings, and the special needs of your students. With you and your needs in mind, then, we have put together some ideas and recommendations that you can use in preparing your public speaking course.

The instructor's manual for *Public Speaking in a Diverse Society* is divided into seven parts. All 1,100+ examination questions are published under separate cover and available in computerized format.

- **Part 1** provides an overview of the course, including a sample syllabus, topic outlines and assignments for organizing the course based on either a semester or quarter system, and general tips and strategies for new teachers.

- **Part 2** suggests ways to deal sensitively with cultural issues in this course. We provide activities for increasing cultural awareness and we recommend strategies to help create a *safe* climate for discussing intercultural issues and concerns.

- **Part 3** combines student-oriented learning objectives for each chapter in the text, extended outlines for each chapter, and a variety of in-class activities that encourage students to translate theory and research into practice. We also provide a list of questions to stimulate classroom interaction and interest as well as an annotated reading list appropriate for each chapter.

- **Part 4** presents our philosophy of evaluating students' oral performances along with a series of speech evaluation forms that you can use or modify for your own critiques of students' presentations.

- **Part 5** provides a detailed analysis of the student speeches presented in the videotape accompanying the text.

- **Part 6** is concerned with the evaluation of students and teachers. Included in this section is a discussion of how to write your own lecture-based examination questions for objective and essay testing; how to take the subjectivity out of grading; how to assign grades; and how to measure effective teaching. It also provides a reference list.

- **Part 7** provides transparency masters that you can use to teach difficult principles and concepts from each chapter.

We hope that this organization will allow you to locate and use the information provided quickly and easily. We wish you and your students an enjoyable, stimulating course!

PART 1
ORGANIZING THE COURSE

SAMPLE COURSE SYLLABUS

Course Description

Students learn skills and strategies designed to prepare and deliver informative and persuasive speeches. Special consideration is given to adapting communication styles and content to diverse co-cultural speakers and audiences. The course includes practice in public speaking.

Course Objectives/Rationale

At one time or another, each of you will be called upon to stand before a group and deliver information, argue a position, present an award, introduce a guest speaker, or honor a special event or occasion. At these times, it is important that you command the audience's attention, present yourself as credible, represent your position clearly and accurately, and speak with conviction.

In this course, we contend that audiences and speakers live and interact within a multicultural society. As such, we need to be sensitive to the unique communication demands of co-culturally diverse groups living and speaking in our communities today. This course will examine both the speaker and the audience as members of co-cultures— cultures that may be similar but often fail to overlap as much as we might like (or believe). Speakers must recognize their own ethnocentrism; adapt to the co-cultural affiliations of their audience; and be sensitive to verbal and nonverbal symbols that may offend, alienate, be misunderstood, and so on.

This is *not* a course about how to write a speech. It *is* a course about communicating in public contexts. Consequently, you will be asked to present to your peers a number of speeches. In this class, we take the point of view that students need confidence to succeed in public speaking. This confidence is a direct result of understanding the information presented in the text and lectures as well as practicing the skills in application assignments. If you are one of many students who are a little uncomfortable (or worse) about having to speak in front of an audience, this course should lessen those fears. If you are a student for whom English is a second, not a first, language, this course will provide you with a safe environment in which to practice your skills and reduce your fears as well.

Instructor: Sidonie Squier (Insert your name.)
Office hours: MWF 1–2:00 PM
(Every university has its own policy; check with your department.)
Office phone: (310) 892-9048 (Insert your campus/office phone number.)

Text: Kearney, P. & Plax, T. G. (1995). *Public speaking in a diverse society.* Mountain View, CA: Mayfield.

Student Learning Objectives:

1. Students will learn how to construct (research, outline, and organize) public speeches for delivery to diverse co-cultural audiences.

2. Students will be able to deliver informative, persuasive, and specialized speeches to audiences representing diverse co-cultural affiliations.

3. Besides developing speaker skills and sensitivities, students will develop analytical skills and active critical listening skills.

4. Students will learn how to successfully reduce and manage their apprehension about communicating in public contexts.

5. Students will become sensitive to audience and speaker characteristics that are influenced by co-cultural affiliations.

6. Students will become aware of their own tendency to be ethnocentric and learn to avoid being stereotypic in their responses to others.

Course Requirements

Attendance

You are expected to attend all classes. Absences require a physician's verification to be excused. Each unexcused absence will result in a reduction of 5 attendance points. The maximum reduction is 20.

You MUST call if an emergency prevents you from giving a speech on an assigned date. A grade of "0" will be assigned if you miss your scheduled day without a physician's verification for an absence.

Do not be late to class (especially classes that include speeches). Walking into class late disrupts the presenter; be courteous. Coming to class late or leaving early will be counted as an absence for the entire class period.

(This is a sample attendance policy; you may want to check your department's policy on attendance and revise accordingly.)

Readings

Daily reading assignments from the text are listed on the course schedule attached. Read the material *before* you come to class.

Exams

Three exams with multiple-choice, true-false, and short-answer essay questions will be given. Each exam will cover readings from the text and lectures from class.

Speeches

There will be three major and four minor speeches. Each speech will build upon the previous one. This incremental method is based on the idea that a complex activity (like public speaking) is best learned in small units of instruction. When complex skills are developed gradually, opportunities for success and reinforcement are enhanced.

Special Notes:

1. You must present your speeches on the assigned day. If an emergency exists, only with independent verification will you be allowed to deliver the speech at a later date (potentially the end of the session).

2. Disagreements over speech grades should be resolved on the day the grade is given.

3. Do *not* miss exam dates. Makeups for exams will only be given for those who provide a physician's verification for an absence.

4. The University's policy on plagiarism will be strictly enforced. Plagiarism is literary thievery. It is taking the words or ideas of another and representing them as your own. Plagiarism will result in an "F" in the course.

5. If you have a physical challenge or condition that could impair your participation or performance in the course, it is your responsibility to notify the instructor immediately.

6. No extra credit work is allowed.

Protocol of Performance:

1. All speakers must be *on time!* Doors close when class is scheduled to begin.

2. All audience members must also be *on time* for performances. If you are absent during any performance day (whether or not you are scheduled to speak), 5 points will be deducted from your final grade.

3. On each day you are scheduled to perform a major speech, you must turn in a typed outline stapled to your criteria sheet. Late outlines will result in a reduction of your speech performance grade.

Grades:

Points Possible

Exam 1.............30
Exam 2.............30
Exam 3.............30

Major Speech 1....30
Major Speech 2....30
Major Speech 3....30

Minor Speech 1.....5
Minor Speech 2.....5
Minor Speech 3.....5
Minor Speech 4.....5

Total......200 points

(The more speaking opportunities you can provide your students, the better. You may want to assign as many as three or four major speeches, but you may also want to assign some mini-presentations such as 1-minute speeches, like giving a toast or an award speech, presenting a eulogy or graduation speech, or making some other kind of specialized presentation.)

Grading Scale	**Percent**
A = 180–200	90–100%
B = 160–179	80–89
C = 140–159	70–79
D = 120–139	60–69
F = 119 and below	59 and below

TEACHING A SEMESTER COURSE

15-Week, 45-Hour Semester Course Outline

Week	Speeches, Lectures, and Exams	Readings
1	Syllabus Lecture Minor Speech 1: Speech of Introduction	Chapters 1–2
2	Lecture Minor Speech 2: Presenting an Award	Chapters 3–4
3	Lecture Minor Speech 3: Accepting an Award	Chapters 5–6
4	Exam 1 Lecture	Chapter 7
5	Lecture Major Speech 1: Informative	Chapters 8–9
6	Major Speech 1 (continued) Lecture	Chapters 10–11
7	Lecture Exam 2	Chapter 12
8	Major Speech 2: Informative	
9	Lecture	Chapter 13
10	Minor Speech 3: Giving a Toast Lecture	Chapters 14–15
11	Lecture	Chapter 16
12	Major Speech 3: Persuasive	
13	Major Speech 3 (continued) Lecture	Chapter 17
14	Minor Speech 4: Eulogy Lecture	Chapter 18
15	Exam 3	

(Depending on the number of speeches assigned, you may want to rearrange your weekly course outline. For example, you may want to allow one 50-minute session solely for the presentation of six or seven student speeches, which are about 4 to 5 minutes in length.)

TEACHING A QUARTER COURSE

10-Week, 40-Hour Quarter Course Outline

Week	Speeches, Lectures, and Exams	Readings
1	Syllabus Lecture	Chapters 1–2
2	Minor Speech 1: Speech of Introduction Minor Speech 2: Presenting an Award Lecture	Chapters 3–4
3	Minor Speech 3: Accepting an Award Lecture	Chapters 5–6
4	Exam 1 Major Speech 1: Informative	Chapters 7–8
5	Major Speech 1 (continued) Lecture	Chapters 9–11
6	Major Speech 2: Informative	Chapter 12
7	Exam 2 Lecture	Chapter 13
8	Minor Speech 4: A Graduation Toast Lecture	Chapters 14–15
9	Major Speech 3: Persuasive Lecture	Chapters 16–17
10	Lecture Exam 3	Chapter 18

(Depending on the number of speeches assigned, you may want to rearrange your weekly course outline. For example, you may want to allow one 75-minute session solely for the presentation of nine or ten student speeches, which are about 4 to 5 minutes in length.)

TEACHING TIPS FOR NEW TEACHERS

A General Overview of Teaching and Planning

As a rule, many teachers are trained in subject or content competencies within their area of study, but few are required to have any formal background in teaching skills (McKeachie, 1986). Good and Brophy (1987) state that "many teachers fail to fulfill their potential . . . , not because they do not know the subject matter, but because they do not understand students or classrooms" (p. 3). They argue that more attention is needed in studying "action systems knowledge" rather than "subject matter knowledge." Action systems knowledge refers to *teaching* skills such as planning lessons, making decisions about lesson pace, explaining material clearly, and responding to individual differences in how students learn (Leinhardt & Smith, 1984, cited in Good & Brophy, 1987). In other words, there's more to teaching than the what of content; we must also pay attention to how we relate that content to our students. We may all have a lot to teach, to say to our students, but we must also learn how to communicate what we know in our efforts to become more effective at what we do.

This section includes some general teaching tips or suggestions that will enable beginning teachers of the course to enter the classroom organized and prepared to meet the challenges of instruction. The key to good instruction is the ability to communicate effectively. Fortunately, that's our profession. Communication professionals like us have a jumpstart on teaching. Importantly, because we are communication specialists, our students *expect* us to be excellent public speakers and to provide public speaking role models for them to emulate. Every time we enter the classroom, then, we must remember to practice all that we know about public speaking.

Learning Domains and Learning Objectives

Learning Domains

Categories of learning can be grouped into three major categories: cognitive, affective, and psychomotor. These areas (or "domains," as they are generally called) are widely referred to in the literature that discusses learning objectives. Understanding the levels within each domain is important when planning a unit of instruction (Kemp, 1985). For your convenience, we have provided for each text chapter a list of learning objectives that assess all three domains. Teaching public speaking requires that you teach cognitive principles and engage students in a variety of public speaking skills assignments. To develop affect, or liking for the course (and for you), you will also want your students to become involved in a variety of experiential learning activities. To help you develop a better understanding of how to use learning objectives, we have provided this brief overview on learning domains and objectives.

The cognitive domain focuses on intellectual abilities and skills. The six cognitive objectives are ordered in a hierarchy from simple to complex types of learning: knowledge (for example, list the three goals of informative speaking); comprehension (understand the difference between informative and persuasive speaking); application (write an original informative speech); analysis (identify the type of logic employed in a given speech); synthesis (provide alternative logic patterns to the same speech); and evaluation (tell why a particular speech is good or bad) (Bloom, Engelhart, Frost, Hill, & Krathwohl, 1956). Teachers tend to test the cognitive area more often as grade level increases. By the time students are in college, they are tested almost entirely on learning that occurs in this domain.

The affective domain focuses on students' attitudes and emphasizes the development of appreciation through changes in interests, attitudes, and values. That is, the objectives in the affective domain range from low levels of enjoyment or liking to higher levels of wanting to learn even more and applying the learning to other areas (Krathwohl, Bloom, & Masia,

1956). The hierarchy in the affective domain includes: receiving, or attending to something (taking notes from lecture); responding, or showing some new behavior as a result of experience (taking a deep breath and looking at the audience before speaking); valuing, or showing some involvement or commitment (joining the debate team); integrating a new value into one's general set of values (recognizing that reasoning and evidence are critical); and acting consistently with the new value (using reasoning and evidence in the speech) (Woolfolk & McCune-Nicolich, 1984). Unlike the cognitive domain, instruction in the affective domain is rarely strategically planned. However, students are likely to learn cognitively when they are predisposed to like what they learn as well (Kearney & McCroskey, 1980). By internalizing the value of specific content, students also tend to learn content—in other words, they meet cognitive objectives. Furthermore, with an affective orientation, students tend to develop positive attitudes toward the course, the course content, and the teacher. Consequently, teachers need to *plan* to enhance students' willingness or affective orientation to learn.

The psychomotor domain of learning focuses on developing particular performance abilities (in this case, public speaking skills). Psychomotor outcomes include reflex movements (nonverbal adaptors); fundamental or inherent movements (walking from one end of the stage to the other); perceptual abilities (selectively ignoring negative feedback from hecklers in the audience); physical abilities (sustaining eye contact while under pressure); skilled movements (expansive use of gestures); and nondiscursive communication (purposeful gestures) (Harrow, 1972). For students to master psychomotor learning, instruction must be specifically directed toward the development of these and other public speaking skills. In skills-oriented communication courses, attention should be focused on psychomotor outcomes of speech delivery, listening, and other verbal and nonverbal skills.

Because all three learning domains typically occur simultaneously, teachers need to recognize the importance of each outcome. Instruction should be targeted across all three domains and result in a change in cognitive, affective, and psychomotor outcomes.

Learning Objectives

When instruction is based on the domains of learning, learning objectives should specifically define the behavior desired (or required) of the student. Psychomotor objectives focus on observable changes, such as what the learner will be able to do: lean forward, engage in eye contact, use illustrators, or decrease the use of adaptors. Cognitive objectives are usually stated in terms of internal changes, such as understand, recognize, create, or apply. Nevertheless, both types of objectives are simply descriptions of changes in learners (Woolfolk & McCune-Nicolich, 1984). Therefore, if a student has learned, he or she will be able to demonstrate the defined behavior.

Learning objectives serve several purposes: First, they provide a useful method of organizing course content; second, they prescribe the level and type of learning requested from the student; and third, they assist in evaluation and test construction (Woolfolk & McCune-Nicolich, 1984). Additional studies have found that objectives serve as cues for learners to attend to relevant, as opposed to irrelevant or accidental, information. (Kaplan, 1974; Kaplan & Rothkopf, 1974; Kaplan & Simmons, 1974; Rothkopf & Kaplan, 1972; cited in Lashbrook & Wheeless, 1978). Popham and Baker (1970) suggested that objectives may help increase student achievement while decreasing uncertainty and behavior problems. In summary, learning objectives clearly specify to the learner what is to be learned, how it is to be learned, and how he or she can be expected to be evaluated. Having a clear idea of what to focus on, students are more likely to spend more time studying or practicing relevant skills. Therefore, they are more likely to achieve the goals specified in the objectives (Woolfolk & McCune-Nicolich, 1984). Through such organization, the teacher and the students are better able to focus their attention and effort toward instruction and learning. Finally, evaluating instructor effectiveness and student learning becomes easier and more precise.

Writing learning objectives involves formulating a precise statement that answers the question "What should the learner have learned or be able to do upon completing the unit or chapter?" It is important to ask yourself this question each time you start to write an objective. To answer the question, it is necessary to write each learning objective with an *action verb* ("to name," "to look," "to compare"), followed by the object of that action ("to name the parts of an informative speech"). In some cases you may want to be more specific by indicating the performance standard or any conditions under which evaluation will take place. For example: "The student should be able to name the parts of an informative speech in order [performance standard] with 100 percent accuracy [conditions of evaluation]." In many cases, the performance standards and conditions of evaluation are understood by the teacher and the learner.

Testing and Evaluation

Tests are a common method of evaluation. In public speaking courses, exams comprise approximately half of students' total evaluation (speaking assignments typically comprise the other half). Students in public speaking often misunderstand the need to test their knowledge of speaking principles, concepts, and processes, preferring that their evaluation be based solely on oral performance. Be sure to provide students with a rationale for testing cognitive learning in addition to public speaking skills. Tell them that it's important to know *why* or explain *how* particular communication skills and techniques work or fail to work. You might also explain that exams actually help some students, particularly those who are highly apprehensive, pass the course successfully.

Objective questions such as multiple-choice, true-false, matching, and short answer are effective for measuring knowledge and comprehension. Because such questions limit the number of possible interpretations at these lower cognitive levels, responses are often easier to grade. Unfortunately, this is not the case for evaluating essays. Even so, we like to use some essay questions because they effectively measure higher order learning of application, synthesis, and evaluation. It's a good idea to provide a *mix* of question types; in this way, students who are good at one type of test but poor at another will have multiple opportunities to show what they know.

The psychomotor domain can be assessed through the demonstration of skills. Public speaking instructors should rely on some sort of objective criteria that specifies particular skills to be attained. It's a good idea to give students your skills-based criteria while they are still in the process of preparing their presentations. In this way, they can optimize their chances of doing exactly what you want. In Part 4, we provide a variety of criteria sheets that you can use or modify in your evaluation of different types of student speeches.

Learning in the affective domain is also important to measure. Surveys and other types of more informal feedback are effective means of gathering such information. In each chapter of the book, we provide a self-report assessment that students can complete. We recommend that students complete these assessments anonymously as confidentiality ensures more accurate responses. You can use their responses to stimulate more general classroom interaction.

All methods of evaluation are made easier when objectives are used to specify the expected learning outcomes. Specific test questions derived from learning objectives can be easily developed. It is also important for testing to occur frequently. Frequent tests encourage the retention of information and appear to be more effective than a comparable amount of time spent reviewing and studying material (Nungester & Duchastel, 1982). Tests and other forms of evaluation (homework) indicate whether or not you have successfully taught. In turn, feedback from you as the teacher allows students to determine whether or not they have learned. Learning is enhanced by *immediate* feedback (Nash, Richmond, & Andriate, 1984; Woolfolk & McCune-Nicolich, 1984). That is, it is important to return examinations and hand speech critiques to your students very soon after students complete their work (ASAP!).

Anxiety, an additional issue that concerns both students and teachers, is related to evaluation and feedback. Fear of evaluation, though common in the classroom, may inhibit learning (Hurt, Scott & McCroskey, 1978; Woolfolk & McCune-Nicolich, 1984). Often the sources of students' anxieties are beyond the teacher's control. Students may suffer from poor self-concepts, an over-concern for grades, negative reinforcement, repeated failure, or modeling behavior (Nash, Richmond, & Andriate, 1984). Nevertheless, you can help reduce evaluation anxiety by setting up situations that maximize the probability of success. By using learning objectives, assigning numerous minor speech assignments that have only minor grade significance, issuing study guides prior to exams, and offering options within the exam to allow the students to demonstrate their best potential, you can help reduce students' anxiety.

Students are not the only people prone to evaluation anxiety. Instructors must deal with evaluations of their own performance from students, peers, society, and themselves (Branan, 1972; Mouly, 1973; Check, 1979). You can increase your chances of success while decreasing your own level of anxiety by planning and developing a sound and systematic course that includes learning objectives, numerous methods of student evaluation (exams, major and minor speech assignments), and well-developed, rehearsed lectures.

Getting Started: The First Day or Week of Classes

In this section, we briefly outline a list of issues a new teacher may want to consider before beginning the first day of class.

Teacher/Student Concerns

1. Teachers' special concerns
   a. Will they think I'm smart?
   b. Will they know how inexperienced I am?
   c. Will they do what I ask them to do?
   d. Will they like me, approve of me, and be my friend?

2. Students' special concerns
   a. Will this be a nice teacher? Will he or she be easy to talk to and easily accessible?
   b. How hard will the class be? How much work do I have to do?
   c. Will this teacher be fair?
   d. Is this class going to be fun?
   e. How relevant is the information going to be?
   f. How will grades be determined?
   g. How many papers, speeches, and exams will I have to do? What type of exams will they be?

Getting Started on the Right Foot (Forming an Impression)

1. **Appearance (clothing and grooming).** Physical appearance or general attractiveness is one of the most influential cues for initial interactions. Within the classroom context, perceptions of both teacher and students are influenced by nonverbal messages revealed through appearance. In general, informal but well-dressed teachers are perceived as more sympathetic, friendly, and flexible. On the other hand, teachers dressed formally (in suits) are often viewed as being more knowledgeable, organized, and well prepared. For most teachers, it is recommended that they start the semester dressed more formally and dress more informally as time goes by. However, we warn against trying to dress too much like your students; your colleagues, and many of your students as well, will want you to look professional at all times.

2. **Credibility.** Credibility refers to how believable a teacher is perceived to be. Within the instructional context, the believability of the teacher has a major impact on learning. Five dimensions of credibility have been identified: competence, character (trustworthiness), sociability, extroversion, and composure. In general, teachers should strive to be perceived as knowledgeable, honest, friendly, outgoing, and relaxed.

3. **Immediacy.** Immediacy is the degree of perceived physical and psychological closeness between people (Mehrabian, 1971). In essence, immediate behaviors produce reciprocal liking. Certain verbal and nonverbal behaviors have been linked to the immediacy of teachers in the classroom. Researchers found immediate teachers to communicate at close distances, engage in eye contact, smile, face students, use gestures and overall body movements, touch others, have a relaxed body posture, and speak expressively all to a greater degree than nonimmediate teachers.

Verbal behaviors related to perceptions of immediacy include the teacher's use of humor; praise of students' work, actions, or comments; willingness to become engaged in conversations with students before, after, or outside of class; self-disclosure; asking questions or encouraging students to talk; soliciting students' opinions; following up on student-initiated topics; speaking of "our" class and what "we" are doing; providing feedback on students' work; asking students how they feel about class procedures; inviting students to telephone or meet outside of class; and knowing and using students' first names.

Adding Students to Your Class

1. In theory—check your department's policy and follow it.

2. In practice, how do you say no when there's still physical space available? Explain to your students that in order for you and them to successfully complete the course requirements, only a limited number of students can be actively enrolled. Over enrolling the class only shortchanges the students.

Teaching the Syllabus

Explain to your students that the course syllabus is a written *contract* between you and them. Be sure to teach or explain each and every detail of your course requirements! In fact, some institutions require that you go over the syllabus aloud with your students the first week of class to make sure they understand the rules and procedures of your course.

Components of a Syllabus (see sample syllabus)

1. Title of course, catalog course description

2. Course objectives and goals

3. Time and place course meets

4. Office location, office hours, phone

5. Textbook (complete APA reference)

6 Course requirements
   a. Attendance policy
   b Exams: Number and types of questions
   c. Speeches: Number and types of speeches

7. Policy on absences and tardiness

8. Policy on grading attendance

9. Policy on grading class participation

10. Policy on extra credit assignments

11. Policy on makeups

12. Policy on rewrite and respeak options

13. Grading policy, point system, weighted grades

14 Weekly outline

15. Reading assignments

16. Due dates of exams, speeches, and outlines

Teachers' Idiosyncratic Rules

Not all rules and procedures in a course have good, sound instructional reasons behind them. They *should*, but teachers are only human, and some behaviors or practices annoy them. For those behaviors you are unable to ignore or tolerate, be sure to tell your students what you prefer instead. Tell them your special concerns or requirements. You may want all speech outlines turned in to be stapled, late students to knock before entering the room or wait outside till the student speaker is finished, or students to call you by your professional title or your first name. Whatever the idiosyncracy, tell them what you want instead. You'll save yourself a lot of hassle—and your students some embarrassment—if you both understand the rules and procedures of the course right away.

Setting the Tone and Pace of the First Day or Week

The first week of class is often characterized by a lot of administrative duties. Try to relax and enjoy yourself during this period. Be firm but friendly. Get to know your students. Take time to learn their names, where they are from, why they are interested (or not interested) in taking your course. Find out if they have any special problems or concerns. Try to reduce their anxieties about taking your class and about public speaking.

At the same time, give them some information about yourself. Besides letting them know some of your own professional credentials (be careful not to brag, but don't sell yourself short), tell them a little about your own life. Do you have children? How many? How old? What about pets? Hobbies? Favorite local restaurants and shops? When selecting what information to disclose and what information to withhold, keep in mind one important principle: Students like to hear good things about teachers—what they like, as opposed to what they don't like. They like teachers to stimulate and promote a positive, warm, and supportive climate.

Tips on Lecturing Effectively

Lecturing well is a lot like effectively presenting a speech. In fact, we refer to lecturing in the textbook as one type of informative speech. Consequently, all the principles for effectively informing apply to giving a good lecture. What follows are some extra tips that we have found useful in our own efforts to present information in a way that both stimulates student learning of difficult concepts and captures their interest.

1. Put an outline of your lecture on the board or list key concepts that you intend to cover that day. The transparency masters in this manual, for use with an overhead projector, can help in this regard.

2. Orient students to the day's topic by:
   a. Discussing the significance of the topic. Ask and answer the question "Why do I need to learn this?"
   b. Showing how the new topic/information relates to past learning.

3. Define key terms. Give your definitions slowly to make sure that students have enough time to write them.

4. Provide at least one example per concept or principle. Then, have students provide one of their own examples.

5. Apply the concept or principle. This tip is particularly important when teaching skills like public speaking. This can be done through some kind of activity, exercise, questionnaire, or role-playing or by having the students give an actual presentation that demonstrates those principles. Be sure to talk about the actual behaviors or skills that demonstrate your concept or principle. For instance, when discussing speaker credibility, it's important to extend your lecture to include the actual verbal and nonverbal behaviors that enhance or detract from speaker credibility. Then, have students demonstrate those behaviors the next time they stand up to give a speech.

Tips on Facilitating Discussion

Encouraging student discussion in the classroom is often difficult at first. What follows are some strategies that are helpful in eliciting student talk.

1. Before entering the classroom, generate a list of questions that you can ask students regarding the reading material, the speech assignment, and so on.

2. Be sure to ask open-ended questions—those that ask for more than a simple yes or no answer.

3. When lecturing, provide an example that demonstrates the concept or principle. Then, ask students to do the same. Oftentimes, if you generate your own example first, students will be able to think of one of their own.

4. Don't be reluctant to ask students to give examples.

5. Ask a question and then wait. Wait some more. Most teachers wait less than 4 seconds for a student to respond! That doesn't give students enough time to process the question, think of an intelligible answer, and then encode it. Instead, try applying the 15-second rule. If you remain silent long enough (15 seconds), someone is bound to jump in!

6. Direct your questions to particular students—not by name, but by giving one or two of them prolonged eye contact.

7. Target your questions to those students who like to talk—those with little or moderate apprehension about communicating. Highly apprehensive students are not likely to help you out, not because they don't want to, but because they're afraid to. Incidentally, don't confuse silence or culture with apprehension. In some cultures, it's impolite to question or interrupt, but students from those cultures enjoy answering when they are asked a direct question.

8. Ask "why" questions as a follow-up to a story or a comment that a student made. In other words, *extend* any input that a student offers.

9. Ask students to discuss the consequences or implications of the situation being discussed: "So *then* what did you do?" or "What happened after that?"

10. Ask students to share their *feelings* about a particular episode or experience that happened to them: "Did that make you angry?"

11. Ask students to indicate what they gained or lost from their experience—and what they might have gained or lost if they had changed their communication behavior: "What did you gain (or lose) by giving your presentation that way?" and "What will you gain (or lose) if you try this?"

PART 2
DEALING WITH CO-CULTURAL ISSUES IN THE CLASSROOM

Teaching a public speaking course with a focus on cultural diversity differs from teaching such a course without that emphasis. Although exciting, teaching issues like diversity can be problematic: There is always the potential for disagreement, anxiety, and uneasiness among students. Talking about diversity is unexpected in a course on public speaking. You may find some students eager to learn, yet uncertain how to contribute to discussions that may reveal their own unfamiliarity about or intolerance of other co-cultures. Others may be somewhat resistant to learning about and accepting new ways of relating to other people. Still other students may use your course as an opportunity to present their own political agendas. Having taught this course ourselves—and having directed 20 or more teaching assistants in their teaching of this course—we recognize that discussions about ethnocentrism, prejudice, different co-cultural styles of communicating, and other related topics introduce both uncertainty and anxiety. At the same time, we found these discussions both stimulating and worthwhile—and so did our students.

As the teacher, it is your responsibility to manage classroom discussions in such a way that a free exchange of ideas results. Students should recognize and respect one another's contributions—even when they disagree with those contributions. You also need to make your classroom *safe* for all students to speak out and be heard. The best way to promote those objectives is to model the behaviors that you want your students to emulate. What follows are some common questions or situations that you may find yourself in, followed by some suggestions that we've used ourselves in our efforts to create a safe, interactive classroom environment.

How do I introduce culture as a concept in a course on public speaking? Where do I begin?

Introduce culture in the first week of class as part of the communication-based model of public speaking. After defining the concept, ask students to describe their own co-cultural affiliations: What co-cultures do they belong to? What co-cultural affiliations matter most to them? How does their ethnic or racial co-culture influence how they interact with people like themselves and with people who are different?

Begin by talking about your own co-cultural background: I am a teacher, jogger, Christian, female, and so on. Discuss how those co-cultural affiliations are important or unimportant to you, how they influence how you interact with others. Invite students to participate as well.

The first major informative speech is a good opportunity to have students think about and do some research on their own co-cultural background. You might assign the general topic of that speech as: "My Co-Culture." Have students narrow the topic first by selecting a particular co-culture that reflects who they are and then further by focusing on a particular aspect of that co-culture. Our students greatly appreciated the chance to talk about how they share (or not) the characteristics of their co-culture listed in Chapter 3.

How can I avoid alienating students who may overreact or misunderstand the co-cultural styles presented in Chapter 3? What do I say to those who claim that their co-culture is inaccurately characterized in the book?

Emphasize that the characterizations in the book are based on aggregates of people who belong to that co-culture and not on unique individuals. None of us are easily categorized or stereotyped; we are all unique. And yet, we are also somewhat alike. Begin by using yourself as an example. If you happen to be Euroamerican, for instance, talk about how you differ from the characteristics presented in Chapter 3 on Euroamericans—be specific. But also talk about those characteristics that are like you. You may want to emphasize the fact that you know a lot of other Euroamericans who do fit many, if not all, of those characteristics. You might also suggest that those characteristics are more like you than any of the other co-cultural styles represented in the book.

When describing the co-cultural styles of speaking, it's a good idea not to always use the Euroamerican or majority group as your basis for comparison. We don't want students to get the wrong idea that somehow the Euroamerican co-culture is the standard. Moreover, other co-cultural groups might offer an easier way to make distinctions. For instance, it's a good idea to compare Asian American communication styles with those of African Americans—students will more readily see the differences in these two disparate styles of communicating than they would if you compared Asian Americans to Native Americans.

What are some ways I can show students that I respect them as individuals?

First, learn students' names early and use them frequently. Recognizing students by name illustrates to them that you regard them as individuals and that you care about them as individuals.

Second, elicit student input. (See "Tips on Facilitating Discussion" in Part 1 of this manual for concrete ways to do that.) Encourage everyone to participate.

Third, when students do participate in class, make every effort to provide them with reinforcement—assuming that you want them to continue that particular type of contribution. Even if the contributions seem irrelevant or wrong, find a way to reinforce them. A student once told us that her college math teacher told her not to ask any questions in class. (The teacher felt he had too much material to cover to be interrupted with questions.) The student's response was not to return to class again. Don't let that happen to you; learning is more likely to happen in interactive classrooms than teacher-dominated or quiet classrooms.

Fourth, allow students to say what they really think and feel, not just what you want to hear. Sometimes what they say may offend or hurt, but at least you'll know how they truly feel. At the same time, be sure to thank them for their input even if you don't like it: "I appreciate your honesty, even if I disagree with you."

What can I expect from a co-culturally diverse group of students? What kinds of special problems or concerns will I face?

If your class is culturally diverse, as ours generally are, be prepared for students to communicate in class in ways that reflect their co-cultural background. We had one Euroamerican instructor who complained to us that her African American students talked too much in class and were, in her words, "contentious and aggressive." She was certain they didn't like her; because she was always telling them to quiet down, she was nervous that they all thought she was racist. The truth is, she might have expected many of her African American students to be more open, direct, and confrontive as compared to Asian American, Native American, or Euroamerican students. (See Chapter 3 for a discussion of unique co-cultural styles of communicating). Recognizing that these students' style of communicating may differ from her own will not solve her need to have a quiet classroom, but it should reduce some of her anxiety and uncertainty about their motivations.

Similarly, if your class is dominated by Asian Americans, do not expect many of them to engage in lively interaction. You might plan ways to make such interactions happen by being even more immediate, entertaining, and responsive. But if you do not succeed, don't assume that your students are unenthused—their response or lack of response may be a function of their co-cultural style of relating. We've had some students who simply did not emote or interact in class no matter how hard we tried to elicit their interaction. Many of those same students, however, remained in the classroom after class to interact with us. It was important for us to remember that some cultural groups, some students, find it impolite or disrespectful to make comments or ask questions in front of the entire class and would prefer, instead, to speak in private.

Sometimes my students get too intense when a controversial issue is addressed and I fear that I will lose control of the class. What should I do?

In order to manage student interaction effectively, you need to practice both verbal and nonverbal immediacy behaviors. For example, be sure to know and use your students' names regularly; give eye contact, smile, talk to your students before and after class. (Chapter 14 provides a variety of ways to enhance verbal immediacy; Chapter 15 identifies nonverbal immediacy behaviors that you can use.) Immediacy behaviors help to establish a sense of closeness and caring with your students. When you are immediate, you are in a good position to maintain control and elicit student cooperation. And research reveals that immediate teachers are more likely to get away with communicating antisocial or punishing messages (at least occasionally) than nonimmediate teachers. Evidently, when immediate teachers try to desist negative student behavior, they are often perceived by students as doing the right thing. On the other hand, when nonimmediate teachers try to be rewarding and "nice" to their students to get them to comply, students are likely to misperceive their intent as being manipulative. In short, it pays to be immediate.

That may work with some students, but I have others who just don't seem to get the message. They talk out of turn, interrupt others, and generally try to dominate the discussion.

Undoubtedly, there are some students you need to manage more than others—some students low in communication apprehension, for instance, may never quit talking. Students do not appreciate teachers who allow one or two students to monopolize the whole class. Practice being nonimmediate with extreme talkers during class; don't give them eye contact or any other kind of reinforcement. Save being immediate with them until after each class session or until you have their talking under control.

What should I do when a student uses biased or sexist language?

When a student engages in biased or sexist language, give her or him a gentle reminder; help that student substitute appropriate language for inappropriate language. There's no need to use the occasion to lecture the student. Oftentimes, biased language slips out unwittingly; give him or her the benefit of the doubt with a simple reminder: "You mean to say _____ , don't you?" And then encourage the student to proceed with her or his point.

Of course, the best way to teach your students to engage in bias-free language is to practice using it yourself. Chapter 14 presents an entire unit that should help you set a good example for your students.

What about those students who occasionally become too aggressive and target hurtful comments about me or to me?

Practice being nondefensive when students make hurtful or prejudicial remarks. If you truly want students to engage in open and free discussion about diversity, then you must be ready for some comments that may hurt you personally. Rather than becoming angry or defensive, model behaviors that show you disagree or disapprove without the anger. In other words, keep your cool; lower the intensity of your emotions. Take a deep breath; speak softly but firmly: "I'm sorry you feel that way; I'm frankly surprised" or "I'm disappointed; I had the impression you respected how I feel and who I am."

What do I do with those students who make hurtful or prejudicial comments about another student or another student's co-culture?

Sometimes students (like us) say things they don't mean. They may use a poor example to illustrate a point or select the wrong word that ignites others' emotions in class. Whatever the mistake, allow the student the opportunity to correct it: Ask him or her to try saying it in another way, or try rephrasing the issue or question yourself in a way that diffuses an otherwise loaded comment. Whatever you do, don't overreact.

How do I respond to students who claim that their co-cultural style of communicating inhibits them from using exaggerated gestures and eye contact while giving a speech?

Even though certain co-cultures are apparently more restrained in their communication styles, audiences still appreciate public speakers who engage in these nonverbal behaviors as well as other immediacy behaviors. Research shows that regardless of co-cultural background, students appreciate teachers who are more immediate than nonimmediate. Similarly, we might argue that audiences expect and would like other presentational speakers to engage in immediacy behaviors.

Co-cultural styles or preferences for communicating are no excuse for not learning the skills preferred by other co-cultural groups. Effective speakers are those who can adapt to the styles of other groups reflected in their audience.

You might also remind these students that it's difficult for everyone to exaggerate their gestures and look at the audience for any extended period of time regardless of their co-cultural background. At first, using exaggerated illustrators and other immediacy behaviors may seem unnatural and difficult, but with practice, students should find the new behaviors useful and appropriate for public speaking.

How do I respond to students who claim that their co-cultural preference for linear (or configural) logic makes it impossible for them to use configural (or linear) organizational speech patterns?

The key word here is "preference." Any individual can have a co-cultural preference for a particular logic, but anyone can learn and practice both linear and configural organizational patterns of speaking. In fact, some linear-oriented persons often use configural logic in everyday conversations and configural-oriented individuals may use linear logic in giving directions or teaching an unfamiliar concept. Encourage your students to try both logic types; when they do, they may have a greater respect and appreciation for how they and others organize information.

What are some activities that I can use to introduce culture in a course on public speaking?

Between our teaching assistants and our own instruction of the course, we tried several different approaches in our efforts to introduce culture. What follows are some activities that have worked for us:

1. As we mentioned earlier, we once asked students to give their first major informative speech on their own cultural background. At first, students were certain that they had nothing particularly interesting to say about their own co-culture, but with a little research, they discovered that they had plenty to offer. Without exception, our student speakers and the audience found this speech assignment interesting and worthwhile. The only constraint we put on this assignment was that they could not do a demonstration speechon their culture's food. With this constraint, we were hoping that speakers would inform the audience about representations of their culture that went beyond the more obvious and familiar symbols.

2. For extra credit on the first exam, we asked our students to select two individuals (female and male) represented in national television or film that reflected each of the co-cultures depicted in Chapter 3 (Euroamerican, African American, Asian American, Latino, Native American, and Middle Eastern American). You'll be surprised how difficult this assignment is for the class; it quickly becomes clear how some co-cultures are excluded from media attention. Here's a short list we and our students compiled for each co-culture (except Euroamerican, which is well represented):

African American
Arsenio Hall
Louis Farrakhan
Maya Angelou
Denzel Washington
Jesse Jackson
Monteil Williams
Oprah Winfrey
Kim Fields
Eddie Murphy
Magic Johnson
Whoopi Goldberg
Whitney Houston
Bryant Gumble

Asian American
Michael Chang
Yoko Ono
Amy Tan
Chan Ho Park
Trisha Tagasugki
Trisha Toyota
Connie Chung
Dustin Nguyen
Joan Chen
Pat Morita
Kristi Yamaguchi
Lela Solong
Lance Ito

Latino
Geraldo Rivera
Sandra Cisneros
Edward James Olmos
Emilio Estevez
Charlie Sheen
Andy Garcia
Rosie Perez
Paul Rodriguez
Linda Ronstadt
Benito Juarez
Gloria Estefan
Julio Cesar Chavez
Fernando Valenzuela
Ramon Martinez
Mark Lopez
Jimmy Smits

Native American
Wes Studi
Steven Seagal
Lou Diamond Phillips
Kurt Rambis
John Strong Heart
Russell Means

Middle Eastern American
Tarik Aziz
Stephino Demina
Daniel Day-Lewis
Vendela
Bronson Pinchot
Barbara Walters

3. One way to alleviate any potential misunderstandings about the general characterizations of different co-cultural speaking styles is to have students characterize each co-culture themselves. Before students read Chapter 3, ask them (grouped by co-culture or individually) to make a list of adjectives describing members of *their own* co-

culture. Tell them that you recognize that not everyone in their culture will reflect those descriptors, but generally speaking, what makes their co-culture different from others? Next, put the list of descriptors from Chapter 3 on the board. Compare their list with the authors'. Where is the overlap? Where do the lists differ? Discuss how these characteristics represent aggregates of people in a particular culture, not any one particular member of that group.

4. Have students complete in class the scale "Are You Ethnocentric?" in Chapter 1. Afterwards, have students as a whole discuss the questions that follow. For example, you may begin by asking them, What do your scores say about your own ethnocentrism? In what ways do you think you're ethnocentric? Do you think your stereotypes about your own co-culture generally reflect everyone in that group? Why or why not? Are stereotypes ever favorable? Why do you think so? Can so-called favorable stereotypes ever be a problem for members in that group? Why?

5. Having read Chapter 3, students should complete the scale "What Are Your Perceptions of Co-Cultural Communication Styles?" Afterwards, have students as a whole discuss these questions: How culturally aware were you *before* you read the chapter? How culturally aware are you now? Are you surprised at some of these differences and similarities? How well do you think you fit with the general portrayals presented here? How accurate do you think these general characterizations are? Why do you think it's important to learn these characteristics knowing that not all members of any given co-culture actually exhibit these qualities?

6. Have students provide concrete examples of individuals they know (which could be themselves) that demonstrate the communication characteristics of particular co-cultures represented in Chapter 3. Then have students provide examples of people who belong to a particular co-culture, but do not reflect these characteristics. Finally, ask them how useful each of the characterizations are. Why are such grouped characteristics beneficial? Discuss how categories help us reduce our uncertainty and anxiety about communicating with those who are dissimilar from ourselves. Without such categories, it would be impossible to communicate.

PART 3

LEARNING OBJECTIVES, EXTENDED LECTURE OUTLINES, AND ACTIVITIES

CHAPTER 1

A CONTEMPORARY APPROACH TO PUBLIC SPEAKING

Learning Objectives

After studying the chapter, the student should be able to:

- Recognize multiculturalism when preparing and presenting public speeches.
- Explain why completely accurate communication is impossible.
- Identify the essential components of a communication-based model of public speaking.
- Discuss how public speaking is a lot like planned conversation.
- Discuss the origins of cultural diversity in America.
- Recognize the extent to which culture influences public speaking.
- Distinguish between cultural exclusion and cultural inclusion.
- Recognize the need to be culturally sensitive as a speaker and as an audience member.
- Critically analyze and evaluate information.

Extended Chapter Outline

This chapter focuses on the impact of multiculturalism on speakers and audiences in the United States today.

I. The Approach We Take in This Book
This text provides students with the essential knowledge and skills to create and deliver an effective public presentation. It also includes information on how to reflect multiculturalism when preparing and presenting speeches. According to intercultural communication research, what is appropriate for one co-cultural group is not for another. Consequently, effective public speakers are those who are able to adapt to all kinds of audiences made up of all kinds of people.

II. Public Speaking as Extended Conversation
   A. What Is Communication?
      Human communication is a process by which sources use verbal and nonverbal symbols to transmit messages to receivers in such a way that similar meanings are constructed and understood.
      1. Communication as transaction
         The process of simultaneous encoding and decoding is called "transaction." Most communication transactions involve both verbal and nonverbal symbols. Verbal symbols involve the use of conventional utterances or words. Nonverbal symbols include the use of gestures, actions, objects, sounds, time, and space to arouse meanings.
      2. Achieving accurate communication
         To achieve the goal of completely accurate communication, all the source's intended meanings must be decoded by the receiver so that they match. This does not happen because the meanings being communicated are subjective; because people attend to, perceive, and remember things differently; and because individuals encode and decode messages differently. Consequently, words used to symbolize meanings can distort, rather than clarify.
   B. A Communication-Based Model of Public Speaking
      1. The source
         The source is the person standing in front of the group, encoding a preplanned message, and transmitting it verbally and nonverbally to the audience. The source must also play the role of the receiver.
      2. The message
         The message is what the source (speaker) says to the audience. The message includes topic selection, research, organization, and delivery skills.
      3. The channel
         The channel is the way the message is transmitted through space and time. The channel is an important factor in how the message is delivered.
      4. The receivers
         The receivers are the audience for whom the message is intended; they are the listeners who receive transmissions and decode messages. Public speakers must identify their audience. Each audience member brings different expectations, beliefs, attitudes, and values to the event.
      5. The feedback
         Feedback is the act of the audience taking on the role of the source by supplying critical information to the speaker. In public speaking, feedback usually takes the form of nonverbal messages.

6. The context
Context refers to the time and place in which the speech occurs. The circumstances surrounding the speaking event significantly affect topic and delivery.
C. Public Speaking as Planned Conversation
1. Relating one-on-one
By noticing the audience as one individual and then another, the speaker allows personalized interactions to occur. This enables him or her to appear easy, natural, and spontaneous and allows the audience to form a relationship with the speaker.
2. Communicating face-to-face
Face-to-face interactions are common in public speaking events. Effective speakers take advantage of face-to-face communication by adapting to audience reactions.
3. Planned spontaneity
Rehearsing the speech, or imagining the interaction between speaker and audience, can help put spontaneity in the presentation. Audience members expect speakers to be poised, prepared, and confident.

III. Communicating in a Culturally Diverse Society
A. What Is Culture?
"Culture," as defined by anthropologist Edward B. Tylor in 1871, is a complex whole that includes knowledge, belief, art, law, morals, customs, and any other habits acquired by people in a society. The first key to understanding culture is to emphasize the difference between a society, which is a number of people carrying on a common life, and their culture, which they produce and practice.
1. General or "mainstream" culture
General or "mainstream" culture refers to the ability to coexist within a larger society and communicate in predictable ways. The general culture holds the society together into a functioning system, regardless of any individual's ethnic ancestry, race, or language.
2. Co-cultures
Co-culture refers to a unique pattern of cultural features that characterize either a particular racial or ethnic group or any other distinctive social category in a society. Members of each co-culture share at least some similar language, beliefs, attitudes, and norms for communication behavior, setting the group apart from the remainder of the society.
B. Recognizing Our Diversity
1. Origins of diversity in America
The origins of our cultural diversity began when Native Americans arrived 15,000 years ago and continues through today. Ancestors of today's African Americans came in the seventeenth and eighteenth centuries. The largest influx of immigration, mostly Western European Catholics and Eastern European Jews, into the eastern United States occurred in the late nineteenth and early twentieth centuries. In the West, the biggest influx occurred after World War II. A majority of these immigrants have Mexican ancestry, but large numbers of Japanese and Chinese also moved into the West. Recently, we have experienced additional migrations from Cuba, Haiti, and a number of Latin American nations.
2. Diversity today and into the twenty-first century.
Current census data reveals that by the twenty-first century, ethnic and racial groups will outnumber so-called whites in some major cities and regions across the country for the first time in history. That is already the case in some cities.

C. Managing Our Diversity
   1. The melting pot policy
   The melting pot policy was used to eradicate the differences between people by using the public schools to transform the children of immigrants into "Americans" as soon as possible. Anyone outside of the dominant culture was expected to conform to the majority. This policy has come to be criticized for adopting a dominant majority-superiority stance. In comparison with the majority culture, minority cultures were regarded as less significant. This led to the ethnocentric tendency of individuals to regard themselves as better than others.
   2. Cultural pluralism
   Cultural pluralism is this nation's policy of tolerating ethnic differences and maintaining diversity while remaining a unified nation.

IV. Public Speaking and Cultural Sensitivity
   A. Cultural Exclusion in Public Speaking
      1. Cultural exclusion stems from feelings of superiority, ignores inherent diversity, and imposes a singular way of viewing the world.
      2. Culturally exclusive interactions with others may take many forms. One example of cultural exclusion is the characterization of speech patterns that deviate from the speaker's own as "substandard."
      3. A specific Eurocentic bias in public speaking is the reliance on hard facts or statistics to support the speaker's case. Other cultural groups find personal, descriptive, or emotional appeals more credible.
   B. Cultural Inclusion: The Contemporary Approach
   Cultural inclusion refers to the commitment to acknowledge, respect, and adapt to others in our efforts to include those who may think, feel, and behave differently from us.
      1. Recognizing similarities and differences
         a. A culturally inclusive public speaker recognizes that people in the audience may be both similar and different from her or him.
         b. Ethnic diversity plays an important role in how speakers talk and audiences respond.
      2. Respecting individual differences
         a. Culturally inclusive speakers give genuine respect to others' customary ways of believing, feeling, and behaving.
         b. Demonstrating understanding of and respect toward others' cultural traditions suspends prejudgement of others and places the speaker in a position to more accurately convey his or her message.
      3. Adapting to others
         a. The speaker should change her or his own cultural expectations to meet those of the intended audience.
         b. The speaker should consider the appropriateness of words and phrases for the intended audience.
         c. Audience members need to engage in some adaptation to the speaker as well and allow the speaker every chance to be heard.

V. Public Speaking and Critical Thinking
   Critical thinking refers to the careful, deliberate process people go through in order to determine whether or not a particular conclusion or claim should be accepted or rejected. Thinking critically involves a lot of skills, including the ability to listen carefully, to generate and evaluate arguments, to look for errors in reasoning or logic, and to distinguish between fact and opinion. Critical speakers should be committed to selecting and presenting the best evidence available and to distinguishing information

that is accurate, relevant, and up-to-date from information that is not. Critical audience members should listen actively and openly, giving the speaker every opportunity to present his or her perspective.

Classroom Exercises and Activities

1. Have students indicate on a notecard their name, major and minor, year in school, and reason for taking the course. On the back of that same card, have them indicate what major goal or objective they would like to accomplish in the course in their efforts to be a more effective public speaker. Collect the cards; use them to adapt your course to their special needs and concerns. At the end of the semester, return the cards and have students indicate the degree to which they were able to accomplish their indicated goal or objective.

2. Ask students to list on a notecard their anxieties or fears about public speaking. Collect the cards; save them for discussion when talking about communication apprehension in Chapter 4.

3. Ask students to indicate three strengths and three weaknesses in their abilities to give a speech. Put students' lists on the board; identify areas of overlap. Reassure them that this course will help them capitalize on their strengths and manage or eliminate their weaknesses.

4. Have students identify good speakers and poor speakers from the media. Put lists of both on the board. Then ask them to identify the qualities or characteristics about each that make them particularly good or bad. In this way, with the assistance of the class, you'll be able to develop profiles of a good and poor speaker. Notice the extent to which delivery, as opposed to content, is emphasized in their discussion. Be sure they recognize the importance of having something to say!

5. Have students draw a large circle on paper. Dividing the circle into pieces of the pie, ask them to indicate all the different co-cultures to which they belong. Based on the size of each piece, students should identify those particular co-cultures that pervade their lives most and least often.

Recommended Readings

Samovar, L. A., & Porter, R. E. (1995). *Communication between cultures* (2nd ed.). Belmont, CA: Wadsworth.

This book provides an excellent introduction to the field of intercultural communication with a comprehensive overview of this popular area. The authors place special emphasis on linking communication and culture, translating theory into practice, and coupling knowledge with action. This book handles a variety of issues sensitively in a well-written and understandable style.

Lustig, M. W., & Koester, J. (1993). *Intercultural competence: Interpersonal communication across cultures*. New York: HarperCollins.

This book represents the most recent and up-to-date review of the thinking and research on intercultural communication. The book attempts to help readers become more competent intercultural communicators both internationally and here in the United States. Chapter 1 offers the best overview of the labels that U.S. co-cultures currently prefer be employed.

Klopf, D. W. (1991). *Intercultural encounters: The fundamentals of intercultural communication* (2nd ed.). Englewood, CO: Morton.

The author provides a highly understandable introduction to intercultural communication. Klopf effectively considers the important issues in human communication more generally from the perspective of someone interested in becoming effective at communicating with people from different cultures. This book provides the student with a solid grasp of the complexities associated with human communication when culture is involved.

Condon, J. C., & Yousef, F. (1989). *An introduction to intercultural communication.* New York: Macmillan.

Originally issued in 1975 and recently reissued, this was the first textbook published in the area of intercultural communication. The authors employ the notion of value orientations to explain differences in values and beliefs among people of different cultures. This book is a readable introduction to value differences across cultures.

Gudykunst, W. B., & Ting-Toomey, S. (1988). *Culture and interpersonal communication.* Newbury Park, CA: Sage.

This book examines the influence of culture on communication. The authors apply the notion of cultural variability and contextually based communication styles to explain cross-cultural differences in interpersonal communication. Students can use this book as a guide for interpreting the behavior of people from different cultures.

CHAPTER 2

GETTING STARTED:
YOUR FIRST SPEECH

Learning Objectives

After studying the chapter, the student should be able to:

- Differentiate among the four goals or functions of speeches.
- List and define the four modes of speech delivery.
- Identify advantages and disadvantages associated with each of the four modes of speech delivery.
- List and define the steps involved in preparing a speech for public presentation.
- Discuss what is involved in adequately rehearsing a speech.
- Deliver a speech extemporaneously.

Extended Chapter Outline

This chapter focuses on the organization, preparation, and delivery of the student's first speech.

I. Common Goals or Functions of Speeches
   A. Informing Others
      The goal of an informational speech is to change the audience's factual beliefs in some way. Informational speeches should provide the audience with accurate details and clear facts about the speaker's subject. The points in the speech must be clearly understood, and the speaker must seem credible.
   B. Persuading Others
      Persuasion typically involves messages designed to change opinions, attitudes, beliefs, or behavior. Speaking to persuade requires taking a position on an issue and advocating a cause, policy, product, or idea. The purpose of a persuasive speech is to get people to feel, think, or behave differently as a consequence of the speech.
   C. Entertaining Others
      Entertaining as the sole purpose of a speech is rare, but it can be accomplished by using humor or describing an exciting adventure, place, or story.
   D. Specialized Goals
      Specialized speeches are prepared for distinctive events; they are short and to the point. The audience expects the speaker to deliver a brief specialized statement (whatever the occasion calls for) and sit down.
      1. A speech of introduction is intended to introduce or identify a speaker and his or her topic to the audience.
         a. Interview the speaker and learn about the speech topic.
         b. Pronounce the speaker's name correctly.

      c. Help to establish the speaker's credibility by telling the audience why he or she is qualified to speak on the topic.

      d. Introduce the topic of the speech.

      e. Do not talk about the speech. Give up your position and let the speaker assume the key role.

      f. To help the audience remember the speaker's name, repeat it one final time before turning to the speaker and initiating audience applause.

II. Modes of Speech Delivery

  A. Manuscript Delivery: Reading from a Prepared Text

    1. The manuscript mode of delivery is popular because it provides the security of reading from a prepared text. Major points are rarely overlooked, and facts and figures can be quoted accurately. The manuscript of a prepared speech can easily be printed or published.

    2. Drawbacks to the prepared manuscript include difficulty in creating a natural conversation between speaker and audience by restricting eye contact with the audience, speaker's movement, and the speaker's ability to adapt to audience feedback.

  B. Memorized Delivery: Reciting the Text from Memory

    1. The memorized mode of delivery is popular but dangerous. The memorized mode requires the speaker to write out the speech and practice it until the entire text is committed to memory. This approach has all the advantages associated with the manuscript mode as well as allowing the speaker to use gestures, make eye contact with the audience, and move away from the podium.

    2. Drawbacks to the memorized speech include the difficulty of committing an entire speech to memory. Once parts are forgotten, picking up the pace of the speech is difficult. The speaker may have to start from the beginning, giving a clear signal to the audience that the speech was memorized. Like the manuscript mode of delivery, memorized speeches come across as rhythmic and monotonous. Speakers tend to move too quickly through the speech, and the speaker is not able to adapt to audience reaction.

  C. Impromptu Delivery: Speaking Off-the-Cuff

    1. Impromptu delivery is giving a speech with little or no preparation beforehand. Even though people deliver impromptu speeches in the form of everyday conversation, impromptu speaking tends to cause acute self-consciousness. The benefits of preparation outweigh any benefits associated with impromptu speaking.

  D. Extemporaneous Delivery: Speaking from Notes or an Outline

    1. Speaking extemporaneously refers to making use of a well-organized, well-rehearsed speech outline, but not a complete text. Although an extemporaneous speech may vary each time it's practiced, the major and minor points are covered in the same sequence. Extemporaneous speaking is a less formal style of delivery and simulates normal conversation. Extemporaneous speaking enables the speaker to gesture frequently and openly, maintain eye contact with the audience, and move freely around the stage or audience. Audience contact allows the speaker to make decisions about the speech based on feedback cues.

    2. The major disadvantage with the extemporaneous mode of delivery is that without a prepared text quotable quotes may be overlooked and information may be distorted. It is also easier to deviate from grammatical structure and fumble for words or phrases.

III. Steps in Preparing Your First Presentation
  A. Analyze Your Audience
     Audience analysis involves gathering information about the intended audience in a systematic way. The speaker can form general impressions of who is in a specific audience and what general interests that audience might have. Knowing audience make-up and interests helps the speaker choose an appropriate speech topic.
  B. Select Your Topic
     Speakers should not spend an inordinate amount of time choosing a topic. The topic should relate to the interests of the audience and be a subject that the speaker knows something about. Speakers should narrow the topic so that it can be covered in the allotted time.
  C. Research Your Subject
     The use of evidence is important in preparing a speech. Evidence helps the speaker define, clarify, illustrate, and support his or her position.
     1. Personal experience can be an important source of information for the speech. Subjective experiences associated with the speech topic help the speaker develop a point or illustrate a story.
     2. Experts on the topic provide facts, statistics, testimonials, personal stories, examples, and credible quotes that assist the speaker in convincing the audience.
  D. Organize and Outline Your Presentation
     Outlining is a way of organizing the speech.
     1. The introduction captures the audience's attention and provides a preview of what will follow. The introduction gives an overview of the main points discussed in the body of the speech.
     2. The body of the speech describes the main ideas and reveals the supporting evidence for those ideas. The body consists of up to four main ideas and supporting material or subpoints to illustrate them. The body of the speech should be prepared before theintroduction or conclusion.
     3. The conclusion summarizes the main ideas of the speech and finishes the presentation with some kind of memorable statement.
  E. Rehearse Your Speech
     Rehearse the speech from an outline, not word for word from the text. Practice out loud in front of a mirror or using a tape recorder or video recorder. After a few practice sessions, practice the speech for a friend, spouse, or parent. Make any necessary adjustments based on audience feedback. Rehearsing the speech reduces anxiety and assists in a successful presentation.

Classroom Exercises and Activities

1. Now is the time to get students up on their feet and speaking in front of the group. A minor speech of introduction is a good way to start. Students need to select a partner, preferably someone they do not know. Give them 15 minutes to interview one another and then, for the next class session, have partners formally introduce each other to the class in a speech of introduction. Part 4 provides an evaluation form that you can use to critique each speech. Be sure to go over the criteria ahead of time so that students will know what to expect.

2. Chapter 2 provides a sample speech presented by a first-year student. To demonstrate the advantages and disadvantages of manuscript versus extemporaneous speaking, have a volunteer from class read the speech aloud to the class. Immediately afterward, present the speech yourself—extemporaneously. Then have your students indicate what was good and bad about each method of delivery.

3. Have students indicate what speech mannerisms they find particularly annoying about other speakers (including teachers) they have observed over the years. Next have students identify what mannerisms they themselves engage in that they would like to minimize. Self-diagnosis often results in greater motivation to change.

4. Have students deliver a 1-minute minor speech about a personal pet peeve (e.g., people who talk during a movie, individuals who whine constantly, drivers who tailgate). Part 4 provides an evaluation form well suited for this speech; it emphasizes delivery skills, rather than content or organization skills.

5. Tell your students early in the course to provide enthusiastic applause following every student's speech. Develop a positive, warm, and supportive climate.

CHAPTER 3

THE INFLUENCE OF CULTURE
ON PUBLIC SPEAKING

Learning Objectives

After studying the chapter, the student should be able to:

- Demonstrate why culture and communication are inseparable.
- Define and discuss intercultural communication.
- List those cultural features that make a difference in how people communicate.
- Distinguish between the individualistic and the collectivistic cultural perspectives.
- Distinguish between the cultural orientations of high and low context when it comes to how people communicate.
- Explain how the cultural orientations regarding power distance can influence how people communicate among themselves and with people of other cultures.
- Distinguish between masculine and feminine ways of communicating.
- Understand that speaking style or preference is a function, in part, of a person's co-cultural background.
- Characterize the speaking styles of individuals representing particular co-cultures here in the United States.
- Differentiate stereotypes of co-cultures from unique individuals who represent those co-cultures.

Extended Chapter Outline

This chapter focuses on the nature of culture and how culture influences public speaking.

I. The Influence of Culture on Communication
   A. Understanding Intercultural Communication
      1. Intercultural communication gained importance due to the economic, political, and social need to communicate internationally.
      2. Effective communication requires more than learning any one specific language. It requires understanding and appreciating an entire culture, the beliefs and values of which permeate interactions.
      3. In this book, intercultural communication is defined as an exchange of messages that takes place when people of different general or distinctive co-cultures communicate with each other under conditions where the interfacing cultural backgrounds are different enough to influence or change the process in some significant way.

B. Cultural Features That Make a Difference
  1. Individualism and collectivism
     The individualistic cultural perspective places high value on people who do not depend on others beyond their immediate family. Collectivism is characterized by groups of people who define themselves as part of a particular in-group.
     a. Individualistic cultures are America, Australia, Great Britain, New Zealand, and Canada.
     b. Collectivistic cultures are Japan, Pakistan, Colombia, Venezuela, Taiwan, and Peru.
  2. High and low context
     Context has to do with how much of what is communicated is either inherent in the setting and thus understood by the people involved (high context) or must be communicated overtly through the exchange of messages (low context). Low-context cultures require communication to be verbally explicit, precise, and accurate. High-context cultures tend to be indirect, subtle, and rely on nonverbal cues.
     a. High-context co-cultures are Asian Americans, Native Americans, and Middle Eastern Americans. African Americans and Latinos tend to be more moderate in their contextual orientation.
     b. Low-context co-cultures are German and Scandianavian cultures. In the U.S., no co-culture is as low context as Euroamericans—particularly male Euroamericans.
  3. High and low power, rank, and status
     Power, rank, and status are distributed differently among different cultures. Some cultures minimize power and status differences, others place a high value on social, birth order, or occupational status and political rankings. Cultural orientations regarding equality and fairness influence how people of particular cultures communicate among themselves and with people of other cultures.
     a. Mainstream U.S. culture places less emphasis on power, rank, and status than do many other cultures.
     b. Venezuela, Mexico, and the Philippines place a high value on power, rank, and status.
     c. Austria, Israel, Denmark, and New Zealand put a low emphasis on power, rank, and status.
     d. In the U.S., those co-cultures that place a high emphasis on power, rank, and status are Asian Americans, Latinos, Native Americans, and, to a lesser extent, Middle Eastern Americans.
     e. In the U.S., African American and Euroamerican (especially female Euroamerican) co-cultures place a low emphasis on power, rank, and status.
  4. Masculinity and femininity
     Cultural masculinity refers to the degree to which the achievement of success, ambition, assertiveness, and competitiveness are valued and encouraged in a culture. Cultural femininity refers to preferences for nurturing, friendliness, affection, compassion, and general social support.
     a. Masculine cultures are Australia, Italy, Japan, and Mexico.
     b. Feminine cultures are Chile, Norway, Portugal, and Thailand.
     c. In the U.S., those groups representing a more masculine orientation are Asian Americans (particularly Japanese Americans), African Americans, some Latino co-cultures (especially Mexican Americans) and Euroamericans (particularly male Euroamericans).
     d. Feminine co-cultures in the U.S. include Native Americans, certain Scandinavian American groups, Middle Eastern Americans, some Latino groups (especially those of Chilean, Peruvian, and Spanish ancestry), and some Asian American groups (Chinese Americans and Taiwanese Americans).

II. Co-Culturally Unique Styles of Speaking

Part of becoming an effective speaker is to acquire enough information about other people's co-cultures to be able to communicate respect and adapt to their differences when making public presentations. However, never assume that a person in a given co-culture will possess *all* the characteristics of that group. Similarly, always assume an ethnocentric bias exists in both speaker and audience. Effective speaking requires that efforts are made to suspend judgment of others' differences and to understand why other kinds of people behave as they do.

A. The Euroamerican style of communication can be distinguished in several different ways:
   1. Euroamericans tend *not* to communicate about highly personal topics, although this is more true of males than females.
   2. In first meetings they engage in a period of small talk over uneventful issues, avoiding discussions about more substantive topics.
   3. They take turns when communicating.
   4. They tend not to speak with each other for very long at any one time and are impatient with people who "talk too much or too long."
   5. They avoid public arguments.
   6. They tend not to get too involved with each other when they communicate.
   7. Exchanges are characterized by little formalized ceremony or ritual.
   8. They rank high in individualism; low in context; low in power, rank, and status; and high in masculinity.
   9. They can be characterized as speakers and listeners who are self-oriented, appear to be cold and distant, impatient, unemotional, rational, objective, primarily verbal (as opposed to nonverbal), direct, exact, undisclosing, and seemingly uninvolved.

B. The African American style of communication can be characterized as follows:
   1. The style of speaking tends to be highly intense, expressive, distinctive, forceful, assertive, and openly emotional and often misinterpreterted by other co-cultural groups.
   2. African Americans view interpersonal questions in a social setting to be an improper and intrusive style of communicating.
   3. They are less restrained, modest, or subdued than Asian Americans or Euroamericans in their public presentations.
   4. Audiences are open and expressive, letting speakers know that they are actively listening.
   5. They often strive to make their own personal communication style a statement about their individuality.
   6. As a group, they tend to be highly individualistic; moderate in context; low in power, rank, and status; and high in masculinity.
   7. As a group African Americans are active, expressive, colorful, emotional, often humorous, more nonverbal, distinctive, stylized, open, demonstrative, and possess a positive outlook on life.

C. The Latino and Latina style of communication can be identified in several ways:
   1. Latinos are very expressive when they speak. Expression is often more important than what a person says.
   2. They value elegant speech, using words and phrases that might seem flowery to those outside their co-culture.
   3. They appear social, agreeable, and friendly in public. Arguing or disagreeing in public is considered rude and disrespectful.
   4. They prefer to put social before business concerns.
   5. They value conformity, obedience, and respect for authority.

6. Latinos are a "contact culture"; they stand closer to one another and engage in more touching than Asian Americans, Native Americans, or Euroamericans find comfortable.
7. Latinos encourage traditional roles. Males are expected to be a husband, father, responsible, and brave; females are expected to be protected, stay close to home, and nurture and support their families.
8. Latinos are collectivistic; moderate in context; and high in power, rank, and status. Some Latino co-cultures are highly masculine (Mexican American) while others are more feminine (Chilean American, Peruvian American, and Spanish American).
9. As a group, Latinos can be characterized as amiable, expressive, dramatic, flamboyant, friendly, cheerful, and extroverted.

D. Asian Americans have some common communication characteristics:
1. "Asian American" is a broad term that includes a number of very different co-cultures whose ancestral and cultural roots originated in China, Japan, Korea, Singapore, Thailand, Vietnam, the Philippines, and other countries.
2. Collectivism dominates the worldview of Asian Americans. They tend to value collaboration, conformity, loyalty and acceptance, and acquiescence or even deference to authority.
3. Asian Americans are a high-context culture who tend to hide or mask much of their own emotions when they communicate.
4. In contrast to the Euroamerican style, the Japanese feel uncomfortable when a speaker looks them straight in the eye.
5. Asian American communication patterns are driven in part by their devotion to family honor.
6. Asian Americans, as a group, can be characterized as implicit, understated, acquiescent, deferential, quiet and somewhat withdrawn, courteous, publicly submissive, empathetic, unexpressive, patient, prudent, polite, harmonious, sincere, tolerant of others, and respectful.

E. Native Americans portray a number of identifiable co-cultural patterns:
1. Native Americans are both a collectivistic and a high-context co-culture who communicate in a soft-spoken and indirect manner.
2. As a group-oriented co-culture, Native Americans grow up learning that cooperation, harmony, and getting along are the norms when interacting with each other. Competition is frowned upon.
3. Being a collectivistic co-culture, Native Americans avoid sustained and direct eye contact when speaking.
4. Native Americans are less dramatic and animated in their normal communications.
5. Written language was virtually nonexistent among Native Americans before contact with European settlers.
   a. Native Americans learn through listening, by watching others, and through experience.
   b. They pass on traditions and customs through oral myths and legends.
6. Native Americans rely extensively on nonverbal cues when they communicate.
7. Native Americans learn to communicate in indirect ways. Discipline, as with the Laguna people, is indirect.
8. As a group, Native American communication can be characterized as indirect, quiet, understated, unexpressive, nonassertive, and somewhat withdrawn.

F. Middle Eastern Americans have different social and cultural practices from other co-cultures in the United States.
1. Middle Eastern co-cultures are represented by people from Egypt, Israel, Lebanon, Jordan, Armenia, Iran, Iraq, Syria, and numerous other countries.

2. Middle Eastern Americans place a high value on hospitality, generosity, courage, honor, and self-respect.
3. Public speaking is more an emotional and less a logically organized activity for Middle Eastern Americans.
   a. Middle Eastern Americans tend to be more retrospective than prospective aboutlife.
   b. Middle Eastern Americans are sensitive to others' perceptions of them, and strive to be perceived positively.
4. Middle Eastern Americans have a strong oral culture.
   a. Tribal storytellers once relied upon as recordkeepers are now called poets and serve to interpret political and social events.
   b. They highly value speaking.
   c. They place content and logical presentation second to rhythm of language and the sounds of words as they compose their messages.
5. They tend to be collectivistic; place a relatively high value on power, rank, and status; and slightly reflect a feminine value orientation.
G. Females and males have a number of differences in speaking styles:
   1. Gender-linked speaking patterns
      a. Women are more likely than men to insert intensifiers into their speech.
      b. Woman use verbal fillers to fill in silent, awkward moments.
      c. Woman use tag questions two to three times more than men.
   2. Research does not support the claim that women talk more than men.
   3. Men speak more loudly than women, at a lower pitch, and with less tonal variation.
   4. Women communicate nonverbally more than men.
      a. Women use more facial expressions than men.
      b. Women initiate and return smiles more than men.
      c. Women rely on more eye contact to communicate than men.
      d. Men use more sweeping hand and arm gestures and tap their feet more than women.
   5. Women's speaking behavior is rated as more attractive, polite, and closer to the ideal, but those same characteristics are not attributed to being an authority figure, credible, or in control.

Classroom Exercises and Activities

[Part 2 provides six additional activities that you can use with Chapter 3. See pages 18–19.]

1. This is a good opportunity to have students view the student focus group on the videotape that accompanies this text. A variety of co-cultures are represented among the students participating in this group as they discuss a variety of ways that co-culture impacts how they communicate. Use this discussion to stimulate further input from your own students. Discuss how their own co-culture influences their unique ways of speaking and listening. Ask them to share ways they feel the co-cultural styles of communicating represented in the text are similar to—or different from—the ways they communicate.

2. A major informative speech on each student's co-cultural background is a good way to apply the information in this chapter and sensitize students to individual differences in their audience. Ask students to identify one particular co-culture to which they belong and develop an informative speech with two or three main points (about 5 minutes long). Part 4 provides an evaluation form useful for this presentation (Informative Speech 1).

3. After discussing all the different co-cultural styles of speaking, ask students to identify those co-cultures that they think would be best suited for public speaking. What characteristics about that style influenced their selection? Then do the same for one-on-one interpersonal conversations, for funeral eulogies, and so on.

4. Have students identify a recent intercultural encounter they have had. To what extent were they successful in their efforts to communicate? How comfortable were they? How much uncertainty resulted? Is it easier to communicate with people who are similar or different from them? Why or why not?

5. Ask students to list the names of their close friends. Next have them identify their own and each friend's primary co-culture. How many different co-cultures are represented in each person's list? Why do people tend to select friends who belong to their same primary co-culture?

6. Put students into groups of five or seven, assigning one co-cultural style of speaking to each group. Make sure that the assigned style is different from most of the members of that group. Group members should coach one volunteer from the group on how to role-play salient characteristics of the particular co-culture. Then that volunteer speaker should role-play that style in a 1-minute presentation to the class.

7. This activity asks students to identify the stereotypes and attributions that we hold about others and how these stereotypes and attributions may interfere with effective communication. Ask students to individually (and anonymously) write down characteristics that they feel best describe each of the following groups of people: Euroamericans, African Americans, Latinos, Asian Americans, Native Americans, Middle Eastern Americans, and females and males. Collect each set of descriptions and for the next class prepare an overall list of all students' responses (no names!). Distribute and read them aloud, following up with these questions:

   a. Where did you get these descriptions? That is, how do you know what you think you know about these groups?

   b. Do you think these descriptions are generally accurate? Why or why not?

   c. Why do we form stereotypes? When do we use stereotypes? Are stereotypes fair?

   d. How could some of these stereotypes interfere with successful communication?

   e. How can these stereotypes help in your efforts to communicate successfully with members of those groups?

   f. Were you ever treated like a stereotype yourself? How did that make you feel? How did you feel about the other person?

Recommended Readings

For further information on the Euroamerican co-culture, see:

Althen, G. (1988). *American ways: A guide for foreigners in the United States.* Yarmouth, ME: Intercultural Press.

This book provides an excellent overview of what the text refers to as the Euroamerican co-culture. Originally intended to assist foreigners visiting in the United States, the book gives all interested consumers a meaningful description of both general and specific aspects of the Euroamerican co-culture. This book supplies the reader with a good grasp of the primary values, assumptions, ways of reasoning, and communication style of Euroamericans.

For further information on the African American co-culture, see:

Hecht, M. L., Collier, M. J., & Ribeau, S. A. (1993). *African American communication: Ethnic identity and cultural interpretation*. Newbury Park, CA: Sage.

This advanced book provides a thorough examination of the African American co-culture. The authors do an excellent job of introducing readers to what they call the African American experience. Provided is a careful synthesis of current research on African American co-culture, ethnic identity, and effective and ineffective communication patterns. The African American communication style is compared to other co-cultural styles in the United States. A communication theory of ethnic identity is outlined.

For further information on the Latino co-culture, see:

Marin, G., & Marin, B. V. (1991). *Research with Hispanic populations*. Newbury Park, CA: Sage.

This short text explains the often-misunderstood Latino co-culture. The authors prefer the designation Hispanic to Latino, but whichever label is employed, the substance of the book is excellent. The book effectively describes who is Hispanic, the general demographic characteristics of this co-culture, and the historical background and cultural values of this group. A large part of this book is devoted to assisting researchers interested in doing investigations with individuals from Hispanic co-culture.

For further information on the Asian American co-culture, see:

Hall, E. T., & Hall, M. R. (1987). *Hidden differences: Doing business with the Japanese*. New York: Doubleday.

This short book effectively dissects both traditional and modern Japanese cultures. Early in the book the Halls explain the relationship between culture and communication. Then they explain and equate communication in the high-context Japanese culture with space, time, amount and flow of information, action chains, and human relationships. The book also carefully explains the unique aspects of the Japanese vocabulary, their style of negotiation, and their highly collectivistic approach to management.

Wenzhong, H., & Grove, C. L. (1991). *Encountering the Chinese: A guide for Americans*. Yarmouth, ME: Intercultural Press.

This book, intended to assist Americans visiting China, also provides substantial insight into the Chinese culture as it exists in the United States. The authors carefully explain the fundamental values of the Chinese culture. They move on to detailed recommendations for how Americans (or Euroamericans, as the case may be) can more effectively interact with members of the Chinese culture. Thoughtful attention is given to the concept of face-saving in Chinese-Euroamerican interactions.

For further information on the Native American co-culture, see:

Locke, D, C. (1992). *Increasing multicultural understanding: A comprehensive model*. Newbury Park, CA: Sage.

This is an exceptional book for acquiring a general understanding of a number of different co-cultures in the United States. The author effectively explores issues relevant to understanding African Americans, Amish Americans, Japanese Americans, Chinese Americans, Vietnamese Americans, Korean Americans, Mexican Americans, and Puerto Rican Americans. The section on Native Americans is particularly insightful. The Native American co-culture is described in terms of the appropriate designation of the group, acculturation, language and communication, sociopolitical factors, and numerous co-cultural practices, values, and attitudes.

Dutton, B. P. (1983). *American Indians of the Southwest*. Albuquerque, NM: University of New Mexico Press.

In this classic upper-level book about Native Americans of the Southwest, the author explains in great detail the unique cultural characteristics of the Pueblo peoples, the Athabascans, the Ute Indians, the Southern Paiute, and the Rancheria peoples. Both historical and contemporary information is provided about each group. An important distinction is made regarding the cultural orientations of Native Americans who live on reservations compared to those who do not.

For further information on the Middle Eastern American co-culture, see:

Nydell, M. K. (1987). *Understanding Arabs: A guide for Westerners*. Yarmouth, ME: Intercultural Press.

This book, intended to assist Americans visiting the Middle East, also provides substantial insight into the Middle Eastern American co-culture. The author carefully explains the fundamental beliefs and values of the Middle Eastern culture with details about religion and culture, emotion and logic, social formalities and etiquette, social structure, men and women, and the role of the family. Communication with Middle Easterners is given special attention. Similarities and differences across Middle Eastern countries are discussed.

For further information on male and female co-cultural communication patterns, see:

Pearson, J. C., Turner, L. H., & Todd-Mancillas, W. (1991). *Gender & communication* (2nd ed.). Dubuque, IA: Wm. C. Brown.

Now in its second edition, this book describes in detail the primary differences and similarities in how women and men communicate. Gender and communication are discussed from both historical and contemporary perspectives. The authors effectively include comparative analyses on information processing, language usage, self-perceptions, self-disclosure, assertiveness, and communication norms across a variety of social and personal contexts. The book also includes a discussion of popular images of men and women as communicators.

CHAPTER 4

DEVELOPING CONFIDENCE: COPING WITH YOUR FEARS ABOUT PUBLIC SPEAKING

Learning Objectives

After studying the chapter, the student should be able to:

- Understand that stage fright or public speaking anxiety is normal.

- Define and explain the term "communication apprehension."

- Differentiate among apprehensive people, situations, and cultural groups.

- Differentiate among co-cultures and regions in the U.S. in terms of the typical level of communication apprehension.

- Recognize the consequences of high communication apprehensiveness in the classroom, in social encounters, at work, and in choosing lifelong careers.

- Identify situational causes of public speaking anxiety.

- Explain why speaking English as a second language is a special type of communication apprehension problem.

- Discuss the three treatment programs available to reduce communication apprehension.

- List, explain, and practice specific strategies that will allow the student to reduce her or his speaking anxiety.

Extended Chapter Outline

This chapter focuses on communication apprehension—its causes and consequences and how to cope with it in terms of public speaking.

I. Communication Apprehension as a Common Reaction
   Communication apprehension refers to fear or anxiety associated with either real or anticipated communication encounters.
   A. Apprehensive People
      Highly apprehensive individuals fear communication in most any situation; this is called trait-like apprehension. Individuals low in trait apprehension seek out communication situations. Most individuals are moderately apprehensive.
   B. Apprehensive Situations
      Certain situations cause even low or moderately apprehensive individuals to become apprehensive and unable to send or receive messages adequately.
   C. Apprehensive Cultural Groups
      The norms for communication apprehension vary worldwide. Some cultures, such as Japan and Micronesia, are naturally apprehensive about communication; others, such as Puerto Ricans or Filipinos, are much less apprehensive.

1. Co-cultures within the U.S. also vary in the level of communication apprehension. Research indicates that, compared to Euroamericans, African Americans show slightly lower levels of apprehension and Native and Asian Americans demonstrate higher levels.
2. Different regions within the U.S. demonstrate different levels of communication apprehension. Individuals in the South tend to be more apprehensive than those from the North. Individuals in rural areas are more likely to develop higher levels of communication apprehension than those from metropolitan areas.
3. Research indicates no real differences between females and males in their level of communication apprehension. However, individuals who display more "feminine" behaviors tend to report higher levels of communication apprehension than people who display more masculine behaviors.

II. Consequences of High Communication Apprehension
Those with less fear about communicating are evaluated positively, whereas individuals who are fearful about communicating are evaluated negatively.
A. In the Classroom
Teachers evaluate students differently based on the student's level of apprehension. Students low in communication apprehension are perceived as more intelligent, dedicated, and enthusiastic. Students high in communication apprehension are intellectually underestimated and often perceived by teachers to have an attitude problem solely because they are less likely to engage in active communication.
B. In Social Encounters
Interpersonal opportunities are better for individuals with low apprehension because they are more likely to be perceived as approachable and fun. Individuals with high communication apprehension are more likely to be perceived as cold and distant and less likely to engage in a variety of interpersonal exchanges.
C. At Work
Individuals low in communication apprehension are likely to select career opportunities that demand a variety of communication situations. Those high in communication apprehension avoid such careers. Individuals who communicate easily generally do better in job interviews than those who are more anxious. Research indicates that employers are likely to perceive low-apprehension employees more positively and high-apprehension employees more negatively.
D. On Lifelong Careers
Individuals low in communication apprehension are more likely to excel in the workplace. They are promoted significantly more often than those who are fearful of communicating. They also tend to be much more satisfied in their work because the type of work they do is generally more rewarding.

III. Causes of Public Speaking Anxiety
A. Feeling Conspicuous and Inspected
Being singled out, with the attention of an audience directly on the speaker, causes communication anxiety.
B. Facing an Unfamiliar or Dissimilar Audience
Speaking before an audience of individuals that the speaker does not know, that holds attitudes different from the speaker, or is from a different culture than the speaker produces communication anxiety.
C. Confronting a Novel or Formal Speaking Situation
Lack of experience in speaking before a group induces communication anxiety.
D. Feeling Subordinate to Your Audience
Speaking situations that define the speaker by status or rank may cause communication anxiety if the speaker is of lower status compared to others.
E. Undergoing Evaluation
The sense of being appraised as a speaker heightens communication anxiety.

F. Remembering Repeated Failures
Memories of previous failures in similar situations are a common source of communication anxiety.
G. Relying on English as a Second Language: A Special Problem
Communication apprehension may be especially high when a speaker speaks before an audience whose primary language is different from his or her own. Research indicates that speakers who are normally not apprehensive communicating in their own language often become highly anxious when speaking in another language.
1. Speakers with regional accents or dialects are often perceived as less motivated and intelligent solely because they pronounce words in an unfamiliar way.
2. There is absolutely no relationship between accent or dialect and level of intelligence.

IV. Dealing with Communication Apprehension
A. Reducing Your Fears
1. Systematic desensitization
Systematic desensitization (SD) focuses on the physical responses to apprehension. When people become anxious their muscles tighten. SD works on the principle that by substituting muscle relaxation, people can learn to cope with anxiety-producing situations, including communication situations. SD training gradually exposes people to a sequence of communication situations. As the situations become more stressful, subjects use the stress-reducing techniques they have acquired through the program.
2. Cognitive restructuring. Cognitive restructuring focuses on thought processes by examining the individual's interpretations of the anxiety-producing situation. Cognitive restructuring focuses on changing specific irrational beliefs that underlie people's emotions.
a. Introduction. The trainer explains that apprehension is learned and can be unlearned and replaced with new ideas and behavior.
b. Negative self-statements. These derogatory convictions that anxious people often say (to themselves) about the situation or their activities form the basis of a self-fulfilling prophecy. This phase helps individuals see that they have been rehearsing irrational, negative self-statements.
c. Coping statements. Coping statements are positive alternatives for negative self-statements.
d. Practice. Individuals practice using the new coping statements, which have to be developed, lodged in memory, and available for immediate recall when the occasion demands.
3. Skills training. Skills training reverses the causal sequence of the two previous cognitive restructuring methods. It assumes that limitations in people's communication skills influence their apprehension levels. Once individuals learn how to communicate effectively, their apprehensions will be reduced.
B. Managing Your Stage Fright
1. Select a familiar topic
Selecting a topic that is unfamiliar to the speaker takes away from time that could be spent organizing and rehearsing the speech.
2. Focus on the audience
Most highly anxious speakers focus more attention on themselves than on the audience or other environmental factors associated with the event. An audience-centered approach to public speaking is likely to remove some of the most basic fears of public speaking. Approach the speech like an extended conversation.
3. Overprepare. The best way to reduce fears about giving a speech is to spend time planning, researching, and organizing the presentation right down to the last

example or well-thought-out dramatic conclusion. Once the outline is in order, spend time rehearsing and revising.

4. Visualize a positive experience. Visualization techniques require the speaker to see themselves as successful. These techniques can accentuate the positive aspects of a speech.

Classroom Exercises and Activities

1. This is a good opportunity for students to view the student testimonials on the videotape that accompanies this text. On that tape, public speaking students reveal their own experiences with communication apprehension or stage fright and the strategies they use to manage their fears and anxieties. Have students share ways they can cope with their own fears about communicating before a large group.

2. Return the notecards that students completed earlier indicating their fears or anxieties about public speaking (see activity 2 in Chapter 1). Based on cognitive restructuring, have students analyze each fear using logic and replace each fear with a series of positive self-statements.

3. Have students complete and score the "Personal Report of Communication Apprehension" scale in Chapter 4. (Scores should be kept confidential and anonymous if they are collected.) Then discuss the chapter. Students are more likely to be motivated to learn information that is personally relevant to them.

4. Have one or more low-apprehensive students "visualize" aloud an upcoming speaking assignment. Make sure they practice the visualization techniques outlined in the chapter. In this way, moderately and highly apprehensive students may see ways they, too, can visualize a positive speaking experience rather than a negative one.

5. In groups, have students identify situational causes of their own public speaking anxiety—unfamiliar faces, a large room, a microphone or video camera, the teacher making notes, and so on. Discuss how such causes are normal but not to be overestimated. Then have students identify situational factors that may *reduce* their apprehension. Discuss why such factors should be emphasized. (Make sure that you spend more time discussing anxiety-reducing factors as opposed to anxiety-arousing ones.)

6. Have students form groups and identify some negative consequences of being low-apprehensive and some positive consequences of being highly or moderately apprehensive. In this way, students will be able to see why it takes all kinds of people to make this world go around!

7. Ask low-apprehensive students to give testimonials to others in the class (highs and moderates) about their own stage fright. You could also relate an anxiety-ridden experience of your own. Sometimes high CAs believe they are the only ones who experience such fears. Recognizing that others have speech anxieties and are able to manage those fears can be helpful.

8. Ask students to bring in a recent article on communication apprehension, anxiety, stage fright, or shyness to share with the class. Have them present an oral summary (a brief informative speech) on the article.

9. This activity demonstrates how we all selectively perceive and attribute more negative motives and traits to high communication apprehensives (CA) and more positive ones to low CAs. To be effective, this activity should be done before students read Chapter 4. Distribute the following profiles of either Lucy or Laura (not both) to each student in class. Half of the students should receive and read only the Lucy profile; the other half only the Laura one. Ask them not to share their profiles with one another at this time.

Profiles

Lucy: Lucy works in the inventory department of Lauderdale Electronics. Her job requires that she check stock inventory and enter the data onto a central computer. Lucy has been with the company ten years; even though she's never been promoted, she does her job efficiently and effectively. She gets high marks on her performance appraisals every six months and, when asked, she reports that she likes what she does very much. Lucy often eats lunch at her desk, seldom participates in coffee breaks with her co-workers, and does not socialize with any of them after work.

Laura: Laura works in Lauderdale Electronics' human resources department. Her job requires that she screen all potential employees for positions in the company and orient new employees with on-the-job training. Laura has been with the company ten years; she started as a receptionist, and, after repeated promotions, emerged as department head. Laura gets high marks on her performance appraisals every six months and often tells people how much she enjoys working at Lauderdale. Laura makes a habit of inviting different people to lunch with her every day, knows everyone who works at the firm, and will occasionally socialize with people after work.

Instructions: After students have read the profile they received, have them complete the following scale by indicating their perceptions of either Lucy or Laura. These bipolar adjectives can be read aloud to the class; have students record on a scale of 1 to 5 their perceptions of Lucy (or Laura).

	1	2	3	4	5
1.	Cold				Warm
2.	Aloof				Friendly
3.	Boring				Interesting
4.	Dull				Fun
5.	Restrained				Open
6.	Incompetent				Competent
7.	Anxious				Calm
8.	Unreliable				Responsible
9.	Follower				Leader
10.	Detached				Personable
11.	Distasteful				Likeable
12.	Unattractive				Attractive
13.	Annoying				Pleasing
14.	Passive				Assertive
15.	Disagreeable				Accommodating

Scoring: Have students compute their own scores by adding together their responses to all 15 word pairs. Scores should range from a high of 75 to a low of 15. The median, or midpoint, is 45. Scores above 45 indicate fairly positive perceptions of the target individual, whereas scores below 45 indicate fairly negative perceptions. Average the students' scores for each profile and write the average on the board.

Interpretation: Compare and contrast students' responses to Laura and Lucy. Based on recent research that has examined individuals' perceptions of high and low CAs, we would expect students' perceptions of Lucy (high CA) to be significantly more negative (low scores) than Laura's (low CA). Compared to Laura, Lucy (high CA) is likely to be viewed as aloof, uncommunicative, restrained, remote, somewhat less competent, and so on. On the other hand, Laura (low CA) should be perceived as overwhelmingly positive. People should find Laura friendly, extroverted, polite, sociable, a leader, competent, fun, approachable, and so on.

Discuss how easily those negative or positive perceptions were formed on the basis of very little information. After all, why should anyone conclude that Lucy was cold or incompetent or unfriendly simply because she is shy? By the same token, why should anyone conclude that Laura is more competent, credible, accommodating, or responsible than Lucy just because Laura is talkative and outgoing? In other words, our perceptions may not be fair, and we know they certainly aren't all that objective.

Recommended Readings

Richmond, V. P., & McCroskey, J. C. (1985). *Communication: Apprehension, avoidance, and effectiveness* (3rd ed.). Scottsdale, AZ: Gorsuch Scarisbrick.

This short text provides probably the best overview of the research and thinking on communication apprehension to date. Intended for laypersons and educators, it offers explanations of shyness, communication apprehension, and unwillingness to communicate. Characteristics and perceptions associated with communication apprehension are addressed along with a variety of alternative approaches that can help reduce individuals' apprehensions about communicating. The book is written with the practitioner in mind.

Daly, J. C., & McCroskey, J. C. (Eds.) (1984). *Avoiding communication: Shyness, reticence and communication apprehension*. Beverly Hills, CA: Sage.

Although out of print, this book is worth obtaining for your library. The contributing authors are doing (or did) most of the major research in the area of communication apprehension and avoidance. A number of these chapters appear in the references of our textbook.

McCroskey, J. C. (1982). Oral communication apprehension: A reconceptualization. In M. Burgoon (Ed.), *Communication yearbook six* (pp. 136–170). Beverly Hills, CA: Sage.

Although now somewhat dated, this essay was once considered a state-of-the-art report on communication apprehension. It offers suggestions for researchers interested in investigating the topic further. In addition, it presents a thorough discussion of the effects of apprehension on communication behavior.

Daly, J. A., Vangelisti, A. L., Neel, H. L., & Cavanaugh, P. D. (1989). Pre-performance concerns associated with public speaking anxiety. *Communication Quarterly, 37,* 39–53.

This research report is a good example of the hundreds of studies on communication apprehension that have been published. Particularly relevant to our chapter, this article examines *public speaking* anxiety, noting the research that still remains to be done in the area. The findings of this study are reviewed in our chapter.

CHAPTER 5

SPEAKER SELF-PRESENTATION

Learning Objectives

After studying the chapter, the student should be able to:

- Demonstrate the power of first impressions.
- Explain how first impressions are formed and why they are formed so quickly.
- Define and explain the concept of impression management.
- Discuss the idea of presentation of self.
- Define and explain the concept of selective perception.
- Explain the influence of co-culture on the formation of first impressions.
- Develop a plan to present herself or himself as an effective public speaker.
- Define and explain credibility and its relationship to speaker self-presentation.
- List and differentiate among the five dimensions of speaker credibility.
- Demonstrate how he or she can increase audience perceptions of credibility as a public speaker.

Extended Chapter Outline

This chapter focuses on the role of speaker self-presentation in determining the effectiveness of a public speaker.

I. The Power of First Impressions
   A. The Impression-Formation Process
      1. First impressions are formed quickly. Based on research by Solomon Asch, what is learned first about a person influences how people will perceive subsequent information about him or her.
      2. First impressions are easily generalized. Further research by Asch showed that if a person was thought to have one set of favorable qualities, subjects believed that she or he probably had other favorable qualities.
      3. Some characteristics are more important than others. Salient characteristics serve as a dominant attribute around which people construct a pattern of initial impressions.
   B. Selectively Perceiving What's Salient and What's Not
      Perception refers to the process of making sense of or attaching meaning to some aspect of reality that has been apprehended by the senses. Selectivity refers to choosing, selecting, distorting, and assigning meaning to information from others.
      1. The impact of stereotypes
         Impressions formed from observable indicators such as body shape, height, and skin color are often stereotypic, based on ethnocentric or chauvinistic biases.

2. The influence of co-culture
   Characteristics that might be perceived as salient to one co-culture might not be as important to another co-culture.

II. Effective Speaker Self-Presentation
   The self refers to the pattern of beliefs, meanings, and understandings that each of us has developed concerning our own nature and worth as a human being. Presentation of self involves encoding and sending verbal and nonverbal messages to others about what kind of person you are. Impression management refers to a planned communication strategy that transmits verbal and nonverbal messages deliberately designed to create a particular set of impressions.
   A. Presenting Yourself to Diverse Audiences
      Effective speaker self-presentation anticipates the selective perceptions audience members will use in evaluating the speaker and taking steps to ensure that the characteristics they focus on are positive.
   B. Developing a Preliminary Game Plan
      1. Consider your audience
         Include audience characteristics, such as co-cultural affiliation, age, occupation, sex, and organizational membership in developing a self-presentation plan.
      2. Appraise the physical setting
         The physical setting affects the audience's perception of the speaker.
      3. Use all available communication channels
         Consider both verbal and nonverbal messages.
      4. Present yourself honestly
         Dishonesty is spotted easily in all co-cultures and undermines speaker credibility.

III. Establishing Speaker Credibility
   Speaker credibility refers to the degree to which the audience feels that a speaker is believable and trustworthy and that the messages he or she is transmitting are truthful.
   A. Demonstrate Competence
      Speaker competence refers to how much valid information the speaker is perceived to command about the issue under discussion.
      1. Use precise language
         Use technical or special terminology characteristic of the subject, but include a clear definition. Using redundancy when defining new terms helps to clarify their meaning.
      2. Include oral footnotes
         Reference the sources of evidence used to support the assertions made in the speech.
      3. Admit your ignorance
         Admit to the audience when the answer to a question is unknown. This protects the speaker from being discredited and can boost the audience's perception of speaker competence.
      4. Look competent
         Appropriate dress varies from audience to audience. Based on the speech topic, assess the audience and dress the part.
      5. Arrange a validating introduction
         A brief introduction of the speaker's background is important to establishing credibility.
   B. Generate Trust
      A speaker must be considered as trustworthy—good, decent, and honest—to be considered credible. Perceptions of trust are socially established and validated. Social validation is based on the judgments of others rather than objective facts about the speaker. If trust is violated, it is rarely reestablished, and speaker credibility is diminished.

C. Exhibit Composure

Appearing composed—calm, cool, and collected—increases speaker credibility. Rehearsing the presentation enhances speaker composure. Avoid mannerisms such as pacing and fidgeting that communicate nervousness and tension. Practice using natural gestures, occasionally slowing the rate of the speech, using direct eye contact with the audience, and smiling.

D. Communicate Sociability

Perceptions of sociability are based on how congenial a person seems to be. Communicating sociability requires nonverbal behaviors that communicate physical or psychological closeness. These behaviors include eye contact, smiling, head-nodding, decreased distance. Referring to the audience in a familiar or intimate fashion helps establish sociability.

E. Display Extroversion

Extroversion refers to the degree to which someone is outgoing, people-oriented, talkative, and gregarious. Extroverts are perceived more positively than introverts in African American, Euroamerican, and Latino co-cultures. Introverts tend to be reluctant and anxious about speaking in front of an audience and are often seen as less credible across all co-cultures.

F. A Note of Caution

A speaker can damage credibility by being perceived as showcasing.
1. Overdressing may be perceived as arrogant.
2. Confessing an indiscretion may embarrass the audience.
3. Being too friendly and willing to agree with an unfair audience damages credibility.
4. Demanding center stage and drawing attention to oneself may bore the audience.

Classroom Exercises and Activities

1. Lead your class in a discussion of elected officials and their perceived credibility. Ask students for their perceptions of various personalities (select current figures). How did they arrive at these perceptions? How do they judge the presidents of the United States? How about vice presidents? Using the current president and vice president, ask students to comment on the five dimensions of source credibility: trustworthiness, composure, competence, sociability, and extroversion. Which dimension is most important for political figures? Which is least important? Next compare and contrast those credibility dimensions with television entertainment personalities. Now which dimension is most (and least) important? Do the same for public speakers at funerals, graduation ceremonies, fund-raisers, and so on.

2. Ask your students to make a list of adjectives that best describe themselves. Next ask students to circle three adjectives they like the most about themselves and asterisk the three they like the least. Divide the class into groups of four or five members. Have students (voluntarily) share with their respective group the list of adjectives they created. Afterwards, ask students the following questions:

   a. How important is it for you to screen or preselect the impression you make on others? How did you do that with your group in this activity? What impressions did you try to create and why?

   b. How easy was it for you to share with the group the adjectives you liked the most about yourself? Do you find that people often downplay successes and achievements? If so, why? What's the difference between being confident and being boastful?

c. How easy was it to share with the group the things about you that you liked the least? Why is it sometimes easier to tell people what's wrong with us rather than what's right?

3. Ask students to identify at least three physical or behavioral attributes that serve as anchors for their overall first impressions of others. For instance, someone may intensely dislike overweight people. Whenever she sees such a person, she automatically assumes that he or she is lazy, powerless, sloppy, and unclean. For someone else, the critical attribute that makes a difference might be smoking. And so on. After students identify their personal biases, have them discuss the validity of those first impressions. How fair are they? Knowing they are unfair, why do we continue to engage in this process?

4. Have students individually create a plan for how they want to be perceived by an audience. First ask them to identify the image or impression they want to create. Next ask them to identify nonverbal and verbal strategies that will help them communicate that impression to an audience.

5. Have students role-play concrete ways they can look more credible to an audience. Form the class into groups, then have each group coach one student volunteer to demonstrate a particular (assigned) dimension of credibility to the class. One group should focus on competence, the second on composure, the third on extroversion, the fourth on sociability, and the fifth on trustworthiness. Each student volunteer will make a 1-minute presentation to the class role-playing his or her specific dimension of credibility.

Recommended Readings

Goffman, E. (1959). *The presentation of self in everyday life*. Garden City, NY: Doubleday Anchor.

This classic book on self-presentation masterfully articulates in simple terms the essentials of the impression-formation process. The book outlines the skills involved in guiding and controlling the responses others make when meeting someone.

Tagiuri, R. (1969). "Person perception." In G. Lindzey and E. Aronson (eds.), *The handbook of social psychology* (2nd ed.), Volume 3, pp. 414–435.

This chapter presents an advanced treatment of the original thinking and research on the process of knowing others. The author traces the research in this area to early studies of suggestion. The general properties involved in perceiving others are discussed in great detail.

Brown, R. (1965). *Social psychology*. NY: The Free Press. (See Chapter 12, pp. 610–655.)

This chapter reviews and analyzes early research on impression formation and person perception. The entire chapter makes interesting reading, but most pertinent are the sections on first impressions, the central trait, accuracy in impression formation, and the self and impression formation. This material emphasizes the important part self-presentation plays in human communication.

Shaver, K. G. (1975). *An introduction to attribution processes*. Cambridge, MA: Winthrop.

This introductory text provides an excellent discussion of how the attributions people make about others' behavior influence the overall impressions formed about those people. The impression-formation process is discussed in terms of how people integrate the various types of information they acquire about others into overall perceptions of those others.

CHAPTER 6

BEING ETHICAL AS A PUBLIC SPEAKER

Learning Objectives

After studying the chapter, the student should be able to:

- Explain why being ethical is a key value in virtually every culture in the world.
- Discuss the importance of being an ethical public speaker.
- Explain how being ethical can improve speaking effectiveness.
- Identify ways that public speakers are obliged to be ethical.
- Demonstrate how speakers decide how to behave when faced with ethical dilemmas or other problem circumstances.
- Identify common justifications that people give when deciding to lie.
- Explain how being an ethical communicator overlaps with being a culturally sensitive public speaker.
- Describe the common justifications public speakers give for lying.
- Explain the various ways audiences can tell when a speaker is lying.

Extended Chapter Outline

This chapter examines ethical dilemmas commonly faced by public speakers.

I. Why Be an Ethical Public Speaker?
    Ethical speakers are those who operate from a set of standards or rules of moral conduct that guide their presentations.
    A. Being Ethical Is a Key Value
        A key value refers to a principle or quality that an individual believes is desirable and that serves as a guideline or standard for behavior. Ethical behavior is a key value for the majority of people around the world.
    B. Being Ethical Improves Speaker Effectiveness
        1. Being ethical and credibility
            Part of being perceived as an ethical speaker is establishing an honest and trusting relationship with the audience. It is impossible for a public speaker to be perceived simultaneously as credible and unethical.
        2. Being ethical as a salient characteristic
            Being perceived as ethical or unethical is a highly salient characteristic because it is a valued trait across all co-cultures.
        3. Being ethical as a positive trait
            Being ethical is a positive characteristic that is associated with other favorable traits. Being perceived as ethical allows audience members to trust what the speaker has to say.

4. The risks of being unethical
   Audiences are sensitized to unethical communicators through the media and are skillful at sensing a speaker's dishonesty. Once an audience determines that someone is unethical, the negative impression influences all subsequent reactions and evaluations.

II. The Ethical Obligations of Public Speakers
   A. Present Evidence Truthfully
      Evidence should be presented in an objective and unbiased way. It is unethical to misrepresent statistics, quote out of context, or represent evidence that is hypothetical as being factual.
   B. Reveal Sources Responsibly
      Speakers should provide the sources of their information, giving proper credit. Presenting information without giving credit is plagiarism. Revealing sources responsibly means that speakers should reveal any questions about the credibility or reputation of their sources of evidence.
   C. Distinguish between Opinion and Fact
      A claim unsupported by evidence is an opinion, not a fact. Mixing fact and opinion indiscriminately risks being branded an unethical speaker.
   D. Respond to Questions Frankly
      Evasive answers to questions are judged negatively by audiences. It is better for a speaker to admit that he or she does not know the answer to a question than to respond evasively.
   E. Respect Diversity of Argument and Opinion
      Audiences do not respond positively to close-minded speakers. Speakers can demonstrate a respect for the opinions of others by communicating a sincere interest in learning about alternative positions, listening enthusiastically when opposing opinions are discussed, and illustrating to the audience that both sides of a topic have been researched.
   F. Carefully Consider the Probable Effect of the Speech
      Speakers must consider the effect their words might have on the behavior of audience members. It is unethical to intentionally present information that is harmful to audience members or to others.
   G. Use Sound Reasoning in Persuasive Speaking
      Speakers argue their points by presenting one or more premises—claims or statements of fact—that appear to lead logically and defensibly to a conclusion. Together, the premises and the conclusion form an argument that supports or refutes a particular position or viewpoint. There are two general criteria for creating a sound argument.
      1. The first premise must be accurate.
      2. The conclusion must follow logically from the premises.
   H. Be Responsible Using Appeals to Emotion and Values
      An irresponsible appeal to emotions occurs when a speaker evokes an irrational emotional response from the audience, one that violates sound reasoning. Relying solely on an emotional audience response or evoking deeply rooted values to support one's position is unethical.

III. The Important Decisions Public Speakers Make
   A. Decisions about Ethical Dilemmas
      An ethical dilemma refers to a situation in which speakers have to choose between two or more alternatives, each of which has problematical ethical consequences. Public speakers are often faced with choosing one value, which means sacrificing or at least compromising another important value.

B. Decisions about Being Culturally Sensitive
   1. Speakers who take the co-cultural affiliation of their audience into consideration minimize the chances that their message will be misconstrued or misunderstood.
   2. Political correctness ("PC")
      a. Being politically correct means that one is concerned about fairness, equity, and respect for all the co-cultures represented in U.S. society.
      b. Being politically correct also means being willing to adopt appropriate conduct when communicating with culturally diverse audiences.
C. Decisions about Lying
   1. Lying is deliberately concealing or falsifying information with the intent to deceive or mislead.
   2. Postulates of the flagrant liar
      a. "Achieving all ends justifies any means."
      b. "Fairness is always beside the point."
      c. "All rules and laws were made to be broken."
      d. "Whenever in doubt or cornered, lie your way out."
   3. Common justifications for lying
      a. Lying to protect others is the most common reason people give for lying when they are caught in a lie.
      b. Lying to acquire some tangible product or resource is the second most frequent reason people give.
      c. Lying for the sole purpose of causing harm. This situation is typical when the speaker is trying to maliciously undermine others' efforts.
   4. How to tell when a speaker is lying
      Four of the most easily identifiable lies by political speakers are referred to as:
      a. Suspicious stats
      b. Dubious denials
      c. The tricky two-step
      d. The candor pander

Classroom Exercises and Activities

1. Have students identify people in their lives that they find to be particularly ethical. Then ask students to list characteristics or behaviors that contribute to that perception. What dimension or theme seems to underlie those characteristics or behaviors? (Honesty or truthfulness is likely to emerge as the theme common to most, if not all.)

2. Referring back to students' lists of credible speakers (Chapter 5), ask them to what extent being ethical contributed to their perceptions of high credibility speakers. Is being ethical a salient characteristic for perceptions of speaker credibility? Why or why not?

3. Have students form groups of five to seven members and identify public speaking situations that apparently justify the use of extreme emotional appeals. Then, have them provide concrete ways that people can reduce those emotions (particularly if the emotion is fear). Under these conditions, is it ever ethical to induce fear, pity, shame, or another extreme negative emotion?

4. Ask students, in groups of five to seven members, to list ways they can tell when someone is lying. (Make sure you do this activity *before* students read the chapter.) Then ask them what strategies they have used themselves or might recommend for others to use when telling a lie. For most people, how effective is lie detection? Are people better at detecting lies from those they know really well or from those they hardly know at all?

5. Have students form groups and identify interpersonal circumstances that justify lying. Then ask students to make a list of public speaking circumstances that might justify lying. In follow-up class discussion, ask students if lying is ever justified. When? Would they like others to lie to them as long as he or she was able to justify the lie?

6. Have students complete the personal value and ethical dilemmas scales in the text. Rely on the discussion questions that follow each instrument to stimulate interaction in class.

Recommended Readings

Johannesen, R. L. (1990). *Ethics in human communication* (3rd ed.). Prospect Heights, IL: Waveland.

Now in its third edition, this book is a comprehensive overview of the important ethical issues in human communication. The author effectively discusses a variety of potential perspectives for making ethical decisions about communication. This book sensitizes the reader to the complexities and difficulties involved in evaluating communication ethics. It is useful for examining the ethical implications of all types of human communication.

Aufderheide, P. (ed.). (1992). *Beyond PC: Toward a politics of understanding*. Saint Paul, MN: Graywolf.

This anthology is the state of the art in the current thinking about political correctness (PC). The essays attack PC, argue for PC, describe particular PC-relevant case studies, and attempt to reach beyond the current conceptions of PC. Several pro- and anti-PC testimonials are also included. This extremely interesting book is hard to put down! The arguments represented in the various essays are both emotional and rational—and very informative. It is an excellent resource for students of the ethics of public speaking.

Stock, G. (1987). *The book of questions*. New York: Workman.

This book is exactly what its title indicates. Its several hundred questions address important values, beliefs, and critical incidents we all face in life. Each question confronts a particular ethical dilemma where an answer requires making a sometimes painful yet always ethical decision between conflicting alternatives. Many of the questions asked are directly relevant to ethical decisions involved with public speaking.

Capaldi, N. (1974). *The art of deception*. New York: Prometheus.

This is a very interesting book on how to win an argument by deceiving and misleading people using fallacies, overstatements, and misrepresentations of information. It is based on the idea that if you understand how to deceive people you are better able to detect attempts to deceive you. Knowing how to deceive should also help you avoid being deceptive. The book should help students of public speaking interested in understanding what it means to act unethically.

CHAPTER 7

ADAPTING TO DIVERSE AUDIENCES

Learning Objectives

After studying the chapter, the student should be able to:

- Explain what is meant by a contiguous audience.
- Explain what is meant by a media audience.
- Define the concept of audience analysis.
- Adapt her or his presentation to a target audience.
- Distinguish between audience demographics and audience psychographics.
- List and discuss the formal methods for analyzing an audience.
- Understand the differences between formal and informal methods of analyzing an audience.
- Create a profile for a particular target audience.
- Explain the concept of audience adaptation generally and what it means in terms of adjusting to co-culturally diverse audiences.
- Adapt to an audience that is co-culturally dissimilar to himself or herself.
- Discuss the handling of difficult audience members (e.g., hostile audience and hecklers) and speaking situations (e.g., questions from the audience).

Extended Chapter Outline

This chapter focuses on analyzing and adapting to diverse audiences.

I. Identifying Your Target Audience
   A. The Contiguous Audience
      The contiguous audience is the people sitting or standing immediately in front of the speaker. The contiguous audience gives the speaker a physical audience to speak to and provides immediate feedback for the speaker.
   B. The Media Audience
      Mass media allow speakers to expand their audience by entering the homes and organizations of people they can never get to know personally. It is not possible to predict the reactions of every receiver when the speaker's message is delivered through the media.

II. Analyzing Your Audience

Audience analysis is the systematic gathering of information about an audience in an effort to learn everything possible about them that is relevant to the topic.

A. Audience Demographics

Demographic makeup refers to the social characteristics of the audience. Analysis by social categories can reveal beliefs and orientations that audience members are likely to share and that are likely to affect how they will respond to a particular topic, an approach to that topic, and a particular speaking style

B. Audience Psychographics

Audience psychographics seek to determine what kinds of attitudes, beliefs, and opinions people share. A psychographic audience analysis includes the audience's motives for being in the audience; its interests in and knowledge of the speaker's topic; and the audience members' personal feelings.

C. Formal Methods of Analyzing Your Audience

1. Focus group interviews

Focus groups are small group interviews run by a moderator. Questions are prepared before the interview to elicit demographic or psychographic information.

2. Questionnaires or surveys

a. Because open questions are broad and allow respondents leeway in their answers, answers often reveal why respondents feel the way they do.

b. Closed questions narrow respondents' answers by forcing them to choose among two or more possible choices and tend to generate specific answers.

D. Creating a Profile of Your Audience

The information gathered from observation, informational questioning, focus groups, and surveys or questionnaires can be used to develop an audience profile. An accurate audience profile helps the speaker craft a more effective speech.

III. Adapting to Your Audience

Audience adaptation refers to the process of adjusting one's topic, purpose, language, and communication style in order to avoid offending or alienating members of the audience and to increase the likelihood of achieving the goals of making the speech.

A. Co-Culturally Dissimilar Audiences

Speakers can adapt to dissimilar co-cultures by

1. Learning about different co-cultures.

2. Selecting a topic that will be interesting or relevant to the specific co-culture in the audience.

3. Targeting the purpose of the speech to the specific co-culture being addressed.

4. Sensitizing the language and the communication style used in the speech to the co-culture.

B. Challenging Individuals and Situations

1. Hostile audiences

Respond to a hostile audience by finding out why they are hostile and by remaining friendly and even-tempered. Avoid defensive behavior and show respect for audience members' feelings.

2. Hecklers

Speakers should ignore hecklers. If that is not possible, hecklers' concerns should be briefly and sincerely recognized and the speaker should continue with the presentation.

3. Questioners

Each question should be briefly and respectfully responded to before returning to the presentation.

4. Interjectors

   Interjectors are audience members that provide positive verbal responses to the speaker when they agree with what is being said. Interjectors are to be enjoyed.

Classroom Exercises and Activities

1. Put students in groups and have them develop an audience analysis questionnaire that can be used to assess the classroom audience. They can use the questionnaire in Chapter 7 as a prototype. Then have all class members complete the scale. Put averages and percentages on the board. Discuss the implications of those results on topic selection, use of evidence, and so on.

2. Select five controversial topics that could be easily adapted to a persuasive presentation, then assign each topic to one of five different groups of students. Ask each group to develop an audience analysis questionnaire appropriate for their assigned topic. Have students include basic and relevant demographic information along with essential questions that assess relevant psychographic information. After each group is finished, copy each questionnaire for the entire class. As a class, discuss the relevance and appropriateness of each questionnaire.

3. Have groups or pairs of students list topics that they consider more appropriate for women, and those they consider more appropriate for men. Then ask students to write purpose statements for each female-generated topic that makes it suitable for an all-male audience and vice versa. What problems are associated with adapting each topic to a dissimilar co-culture? What issues influenced their ability or inability to adapt appropriately?

4. Ask students to identify an ideal audience. Have them list characteristics of an audience that they would most prefer when they gave a speech. How does (or might) this ideal audience profile differ as a function of co-culture? An ideal audience for an African American speaker may be very different from an ideal audience for an Asian American speaker. Why?

5. Have students in groups imagine their worse nightmare: While giving a presentation to a large audience, a small group of hecklers attempt to disrupt your speech. Ask students what strategies they might use to manage hecklers. What would they do nonverbally? What would they say verbally?

Recommended Readings

Stewart, C. J., & Cash, W. B. Jr. (1988). *Interviewing: Principles and practices*. Dubuque, IA: Wm. C. Brown.

In its fifth edition, this book continues to be one of the best texts on interviewing techniques. Stewart and Cash provide students with a working knowledge of how to structure an interview, open and close an interview, develop and ask questions, and use the resulting information. Such practical knowledge is then applied to a variety of interview types: probing or information-gathering interviews, surveys, performance appraisals, counseling interviews, persuasive interviews, and health care interviews. We encourage you to give special attention to Chapter 4, "Questions and Their Uses." Open and closed, primary and secondary, and neutral and leading questions are discussed, as are the pitfalls associated with phrasing questions appropriately.

Krueger, R. A. (1988). *Focus groups: A practical guide for applied research*. Newbury Park, CA: Sage.

For an in-depth examination of how and why focus groups work, this text is the answer. While the book may give you more information than you will want to know for purposes of analyzing an audience, its Chapters 4 and 5 will help in developing valid questions and in facilitating group interaction.

Greenbaum, T. L. (1988). *The practical handbook and guide to focus group research.* Lexington, MA: D. C. Heath.

Like the Kreuger text, this book examines focus group research. The most compelling chapter for this course is Chapter 5, "The Focus Group Moderator." In this chapter, optimal characteristics of focus group moderators are discussed as well as the most common errors moderators commit while facilitating group interaction.

Plax, T. G., & Cecchi, L. F. (1989). Management decisions based on communication facilitated in focus groups. *Management Communication Quarterly, 2,* 511–535.

This study provides an excellent demonstration (would we say anything less?) of how focus groups were developed and conducted for two organizations. One set of groups examined engineers' reactions to performance appraisals in a large aerospace company. The second set elicited information from consumers to determine incentives for recycling beverage containers in California. Both applications reveal working knowledge of how to facilitate and gather information from individuals in order to develop a target profile and make critical recommendations.

CHAPTER 8

LISTENING ACTIVELY

Learning Objectives

After studying the chapter, the student should be able to:

- Define and explain the listening process.
- Differentiate between active and passive listening.
- Explain how the context of a communication exchange can influence the listening process.
- Identify the listening behaviors of audiences representing different co-cultures.
- Explain and discuss the benefits of looking like a good listener.
- Explain the concept of speaker-audience reciprocity.
- List five speaker responsibilities for ensuring that effective listening takes place.
- List five audience responsibilities for ensuring that effective listening takes place.
- Explain why the four common assumptions that people make about listening are inaccurate.
- List and give examples of five barriers to effective speaking.

Extended Chapter Outline

This chapter focuses on understanding the listening process.

I. Understanding the Listening Process
   Good listening includes paying attention to both verbal and nonverbal messages and is influenced by the context of the communication exchange.
   A. What Is Listening?
      Listening involves maximizing attention to, and comprehension of, what is being communicated by someone who is using words, actions, and other elements of the immediate environment.
   B. Being an Effective Listener
      Listening must be deliberately and consciously managed. Effective listening requires the acquisition of skills that help discriminate between what should be paid attention to and what can be ignored.
      1. Active versus passive listening
         Active listening occurs when substantial effort is exerted by the listener for the purpose of maximizing attention to and comprehension of what the speaker is communicating. Passive listening occurs when the listener exerts little or no effort in attending to and comprehending what is being communicated.

2. Listening behaviors: co-cultural variations
   Observable behaviors allow audience members to look the part of good listeners.
   a. Observable behaviors that show active listening vary between co-cultures. Euroamerican, African American, Latino, and Middle Eastern American co-cultures tend to be expressive listeners. Asian Americans and Native Americans are less expressive.
   b. Co-cultures with expressive listeners use nonverbal observable behaviors to express boredom with the speaker. Co-cultures with passive listening styles may appear even more restrained in their effort to remain polite.
C. The Benefits of Looking Like a Good Listener
   Looking like a good listener contributes to effective listening by drawing sympathy from the speaker and by encouraging skills that promote better listening habits.

II. Speaker-Audience Reciprocity
To ensure accuracy, the transactional nature of a communication exchange demands that both speaker and audience adapt active, effective listening. Speaker-audience reciprocity occurs when both sides engage in adaptation and feedback simultaneously, adjusting their behavior to each other.
A. The Responsibilities of Speakers
   1. Have a firm grasp of the content of the speech before they try to talk about it.
   2. Select the tone and style of presentation most appropriate for the message.
   3. Ensure that the presentation is appropriate for the context.
   4. Ensure that the message is tailored to a particular, targeted audience.
   5. Consider the consequences of what is said.
B. The Responsibilities of Audience Members
   1. Exert sufficient effort to listen well.
   2. Seek out personally relevant information.
   3. Give the speaker a fair hearing.
   4. Not overreact to what is being said or how it is communicated.
   5. Help the speaker be successful by looking responsive and receptive.

III. Common Obstructions to Effective Listening
A. Inaccurate Assumptions about Listening
   Ineffective listening may result from making inaccurate assumptions about the process. There are at least four common misconceptions made by poor listeners.
   1. Listening is easy. In fact, listening is a complex effort that requires effort.
   2. Listening is only a matter of intelligence. Actually, listening skills are not based on intelligence alone.
   3. Listening requires no planning. In truth, effective listening follows from having planned carefully, not just from the frequency of doing it.
   4. If you know how to read, you know how to listen. In fact, no research supports the idea that people who can concentrate for long periods of time while reading or studying have good listening skills.
B. Five Barriers to Effective Listening
   A barrier to listening refers to any condition, either in the public speaking context or one that is personal to the audience member, that reduces accuracy in listening.
   1. Physical conditions
      External noise interference physically interferes with the audience's ability to hear.
   2. Personal problems
      a. Physical illness and discomfort.
      b. Distractions such as money, relationships, work or school problems.
      c. Apprehension about listening to people when they speak to us.

3. Co-cultural differences
   Disparate beliefs between the speaker and the audience interfere with the ability to listen.
4. Co-cultural prejudices
   Unrealistic attitudes toward individuals based on a stereotype prohibit effective listening. Prejudiced listeners tend to dismiss the speaker's message.
5. Connotative meanings.
   Connotative meanings refer to personal, subjective, and unshared interpretations of verbal and nonverbal symbols and signs.

Classroom Exercises and Activities

1. Read the following story to the class. Ask students to listen closely. Before reading the story, inform the class that you will be asking them a series of simple questions afterwards.

   At 5:00 P.M. on Friday evening at the corner of Washington and Jones streets, a man came staggering out of a bar. A second man approached the first, apparently to inquire as to whether there was a problem. An argument ensued. The second man pushed the first. A crowd gathered to watch. One spectator left to get help. About 15 minutes later, a person in uniform came and tried to break up the fight between the two men. The disagreement settled down, and first aid was administered to a spectator who was apparently overcome by a heart attack.

   Questions:

   a. What time did the man come out of the bar?

   b. Which man had been drinking? (Key: We don't know if anyone had been drinking.)

   c. Who started the fight? Who shoved whom first?

   d. What were the two men arguing about?

   e. When did the policeman arrive? (Key: We don't know if the uniformed person was a police officer—or if the person was male.)

   f. Who had the heart attack?

   g. How long was it before the uniformed person broke up the fight?

   h. Who administered the first aid?

   i. Where did the incident occur?

   Even though you tell students that they will be tested on the story, many of them still will have problems listening accurately. Discuss how barriers interfere with our ability to listen well. What barriers are evidenced in this case? Have students identify them.

2. Present the following list of phrases to your class. Have each student indicate his or her first response to each phrase using the following scale: (5) highly favorable, (4) favorable, (3) neutral, (2) unfavorable, and (1) highly unfavorable.

   Animal rights

   Tuition increases

   Affirmative action

   AIDS

Gun control

School prayer

Protect the environment

Violence on TV

Illegal immigrants

Raising the drinking age to 25

Discuss with your students whether a person's reaction to these phrases would affect a listener's ability to concentrate fully on a speaker's message. What are some other words or phrases that may distract from an intended message? What other words or phrases could a speaker use to replace or neutralize those phrases?

3. Have students demonstrate in class exactly how a passive and active listener looks. When giving a presentation, which type of listener would they want in their audience? Encourage students to assume an active stance when their peers present in front of the class.

4. Have groups of students list what they enjoy listening to (e.g., rock concerts, movies) and what they do not enjoy listening to (e.g., long lectures, religious sermons, the news). How much more actively do they listen to those events that they enjoy versus those they do not? Why? How does so-called recreational listening differ from other forms of listening? How much effort is involved? At what point does effort become work?

5. Have students list their major strengths and weaknesses as listeners. List the responses on the board. Ask the class what specific behaviors they can engage in to modify those weaknesses and to capitalize on those strengths.

Recommended Readings

Watson, K., & Barker, L. (1985). Listening behavior: Definition and measurement. In R. Bostrom (ed.), *Communication yearbook 8* (pp. 178–197). Beverly Hills, CA: Sage.

This chapter reviews and analyzes the research literature on listening. The authors effectively discuss the numerous definitions of listening and the variables that affect listener comprehension. They also carefully outline the pros and cons of various published listening tests.

Barker, L. (1971). *Listening behavior*. Englewood Cliffs, NJ: Prentice-Hall.

This older text is still an excellent statement on listening. Barker gives an effective overview of the basic principles and perspectives in chapters written for undergraduates. Students are provided with guidelines for improving their own listening behavior.

Weaver, C. H. (1972). *Human listening*. Indianapolis, IN: Bobbs-Merrill.

This introductory book is a solid entry-level work on listening. Materials are presented in a simplified fashion, and the reader is provided with meaningful examples throughout. This text is consistently cited in published research on listening and it is a good complement to beginning public speaking courses.

Wolvin, A. D., & Coakley, C. G. (1991). A survey of the status of listening training in some Fortune 500 corporations. *Communication Education, 40*, 152–164.

This recent study reports the results of a survey of training directors for Fortune 500 corporations. The findings suggest that the training of premanagers and managers in the skills of effective listening continues to be perceived as an important part of industrial training programs.

Beatty, M. J., & Payne, S. (1984). Listening comprehension as a function of cognitive complexity. *Communication Monographs, 51,* 85–89.

This now-classic study investigates the relationship between an individual's level of listening comprehension and his or her degree of cognitive complexity. The results suggest that people who process information in complex ways tend to listen to and comprehend more information than those who process in simpler ways. The study provides several insights into the development of effective listening skills.

CHAPTER 9

SELECTING AND RESEARCHING YOUR TOPIC

Learning Objectives

After studying the chapter, the student should be able to:

- Explain how topic selection depends on the occasion, time constraints, and the audience itself.

- Discuss the advantages of brainstorming as a method of selecting a topic.

- List the sources that should be consulted or considered when selecting a topic.

- Select a topic and narrow it sufficiently for a speech.

- Explain why it is the speaker who makes the presentation fascinating, powerful, and gripping, not the topic itself.

- Be able to clearly specify a purpose for a particular presentation.

- Be able to effectively gather information on a particular speech topic.

- Discuss how the co-cultures represented in an audience can influence the types of support included in a presentation.

- List and discuss the types of evidence that can be used to support a speaker's position.

- List and discuss alternative sources for researching information about a particular topic.

- Analyze research information in terms of its relevancy, recency, and credibility.

Extended Chapter Outline

This chapter focuses on selecting and researching appropriate speech topics.

I. Selecting a Topic
   A. Getting Started
      1. Determine the occasion
         The speaker's topic should be appropriate to the occasion. Speeches for serious occasions should not contain levity. Celebration speeches should not use depressing facts and figures.
      2. Time constraints
         Speakers should know the amount of time they are expected to speak and stick to the schedule. Speaking too long or too little can impair the impression the speaker makes and lessen the effectiveness of the presentation.
      3. Identify your audience
         a. Identify topics that the specific audience will want to hear.

    b. Determine what the audience expects you to talk about and meet their expectations.

    c. Choose only topics that are appropriate to a specific audience.

    d. Identify—and avoid—topics that should be avoided for a specific audience.

B. Selecting a General Area or Subject

Brainstorming is a proven method of selecting a topic. Brainstorming requires that you generate a list of topics or subject areas as quickly as possible without stopping to evaluate ideas as good or bad.

  1. Sources of Topics

    a. Yourself. Choosing a familiar subject speeds topic selection and can cut down on the amount of needed research.

    b. Your audience. Considering the interests of the audience generates ideas for speech topics.

    c. Current events. Schools, community events, and national newspapers and magazines offer a variety of speaking topics.

  2. Boring topics or boring speakers?

Topics aren't boring; people are! Speakers make the presentation fascinating, powerful, and gripping, not the topic itself.

C. Narrowing the Topic

Narrowing the topic prevents the speaker from wandering aimlessly and helps to keep the focus on the specific information being presented. While the process of narrowing the topic broadens the selection of topic ideas, the ideas are specific and easily managed.

D. Specifying Your Purpose

Specify the purpose of the presentation by telling the audience that it is meant to inform, entertain, or persuade. This gives both the presentation and the audience direction. Purpose statements should be clear, simple, specific, and to the point.

E. Formulating a Thesis Statement

II. Researching Your Topic

Gathering information about the speech topic allows the speaker to be perceived as credible and believable. Evidence— facts or opinions attested to or endorsed by someone other than the speaker—is commonly used in conjunction with personal knowledge to create speaker credibility.

A. Types of Support

  1. Facts and data

Statistical or physical evidence can be a powerful tool to support the speaker's position, especially to Euroamerican males.

  2. Eyewitness accounts, stories, and quotable phrases

These types of support make the presentation more personal, sincere, and humanistic. Female Euroamericans and several co-cultures, including Latinos, African Americans, Asian Americans, and Native Americans, are likely to prefer personal examples and real-life experiences as predominant, meaningful sources of evidence.

B. Gathering Information about Your Topic

  1. Rely on your own personal knowledge and experience, which are credible forms of evidence that help to involve the audience in the presentation.

  2. Ask experts directly

Educators, business leaders, and professionals can offer their opinions, interpretations, and recommendations on the speech topic. These people are also helpful in locating sources of facts and findings.

3. Use the Library
   Reference librarians, newspaper and magazine indexes, journal indexes for specialized technical topics, and computerized searches are good sources of information. Source information from the library must be fully referenced.
   C. Select Only the Best Supporting Materials
   1. Is it relevant?
      Relevance refers to the degree of association between the reference and your topic. Information should be directly related to the topic or it should not be used.
   2. Is it recent?
      Newspaper and magazine references should be current. Research from journals or periodicals may be valid over a longer period of time. For teachings that prevail across generations, original sources may be appropriate.
   3. Is it credible?
      Evidence becomes credible when it is consistent with other known facts. Sources of evidence should be competent and well-known as experts in their field. Sources should reflect impartiality and fairness in their reporting of the information.

Classroom Exercises and Activities

1. Have students bring to class the day's newspaper, a current weekly newsmagazine, and the campus newspaper. Divide the class into groups of five to seven members. Ask students to leaf through these news media and list the topic areas they find. Then discuss with your students the wealth of topics that could be developed into a speech by simply reviewing these easily obtainable sources.

2. Form students in groups of five to seven and have them list all their hobbies and interests. From that list, ask them to select speech topics that may be appropriate for this audience.

3. Have the class generate a list (on the board) of so-called boring topics. From that list, have students (in groups) select one. Have them generate strategies that will make that topic stimulating and interesting for this audience and share those strategies with the rest of the class. From this activity, students should learn that topics aren't inherently boring; people can make them either dull or exciting.

4. Have students select a speech topic and then go to the library to find five relevant references. Have students annotate each reference on separate notecards and complete the references in appropriate APA style.

5. In order to familiarize students with on-line search services, assign one speech topic per group of five students. Have them identify four or five key words that they can use to access information about that topic. Send them to the library to search these key words on an on-line service to determine which word is most likely to narrow their topic search. Ask them to list and hand in to you all the relevant resources generated with this strategy.

6. Ask students to generate a list of 20 references (in APA style) applicable to their next speech topic. Applying the three criteria for selecting only the best supporting materials (relevancy, recency, and credibility), have them circle three sources that they would be most likely to use for that topic. Ask them to provide a written rationale for each selection.

Recommended Readings

American Psychological Association (1994). *Publication manual of the American Psychological Association* (4th ed.). Washington, DC.

This manual, better known as the APA Manual, offers a standardized format for writing and typing a research paper, thesis, or dissertation. The manual provides detailed information for writing references, including a wide variety of examples that are easy to follow.

Reinard, J. C. (1991). Foundations of argument: Effective communication for critical thinking. Dubuque, IA: Wm. C. Brown.

This book is generally used for an entire course on argumentation or critical thinking. We recommend reading three specific chapters: Chapter 5, "The Role of Evidence in Argumentative Communication," looks at the traditional use of evidence to advocate a position; Chapter 6, "Tools for Evaluating and Using Evidence," examines both factual and opinion evidence as well as tests that can be used to determine the validity of opinions, and Chapter 8, "Tools for Evaluating and Selecting Arguments," helps readers recognize fallacies in arguments.

Rubin, R. B., Rubin, A. M., & Piele, K. J. (1993). *Communication research: Strategies and sources* (3rd ed.). Belmont, CA: Wadsworth.

This book is for students unfamiliar with how to use the library. The authors take the reader through the steps involved in doing a computerized search. They also provide detailed discussions of how to access and use the various indexes, abstracts, government documents, statistical references, encyclopedias, dictionaries, yearbooks, and a number of other potentially useful sources.

CHAPTER 10

ORGANIZING AND OUTLINING YOUR SPEECH

Learning Objectives

After studying the chapter, the student should be able to:

- Explain why it is important to organize a speech.

- Describe the dual purposes of organizing a speech.

- Differentiate between linear logic and configural logic.

- Show how making sense of a presentation can be a function of a person's cultural background.

- Explain why speakers do not have to organize their presentation based on the logic preferences of the audience.

- Identify and give examples of the five types of linear organizational patterns.

- Identify and give examples of the four types of configural organizational patterns.

- Demonstrate how to organize a speech either configurally or linearly.

- Describe the two types of speech outlines.

- List and explain the eight rules for outlining a speech.

- Outline a speech either configurally or linearly using formal rules for outlining.

Extended Chapter Outline

This chapter focuses on organizational strategies for speeches.

I. Why Organize?
   Organization is a way to put thoughts and materials together in a logical manner.
   A. Making Sense of the Speech for Yourself
      As a first step in the organizational process, arrange thoughts and ideas in a systematic way. Discard information that is not truly relevant. Practice the speech out loud and use the outline as notes for delivery.
   B. Making Sense of the Speech for Your Audience
      Research indicates that audience comprehension and speaker credibility increase when a speech is presented in an organized manner.

II. "Making Sense" as a Function of Culture
    What may seem organized and coherent for individuals in one co-culture may appear disorganized to another.

A. Linear Logic

A speech organized in a linear fashion leads the audience through ordered steps.

1. Opens with a specific purpose statement.
2. Presentation of the basic argument through a preview or overview of the main points.
3. Discussion of each main point in detail.
4. Introduction of evidence to support the main points.
5. Transitional words and phrases act as bridges to connect each of the main points or supporting ideas.
6. Concludes with a summary of all points and, if applicable, a call for action by the audience.

B. Configural Logic

Configural logic includes a variety of other nonlinear logic systems, all of which are indirect. While no one pattern for configural logic is the norm, configural logic requires more work from the audience. Generally, no specific preview is provided, or no listing of the main points supplied. The speaker assumes that audience members will impose their own meaning into the presentation.

C. Co-Cultural Logic Preferences

Culture and language do not restrict how people can organize ideas, but they create and maintain a preference for one type of logic over others. Linear logic is most often associated with formal writing and public speaking among Euroamericans and with people working in the physical and social sciences. While research is limited, it appears that more indirect, high-context co-cultures such as some Latino, Native American, and Asian American groups prefer configural logic.

III. Using Different Logics to Organize Your Speech

Speakers do not have to organize their presentation based on the logic preferences of the audience. Selecting an appropriate organization scheme depends on the topic and the speaker's own logic preference. Research indicates that audience members can make sense out of a variety of organizational patterns, regardless of their cultural affiliations. Audiences reorder, prioritize, and remember information that is relevant and meaningful to them.

A. Types of Linear Patterns

1. Topical

Speeches arranged topically are divided into a number of headings or parts, such as advantages and disadvantages, specific categories, or a sequence of reasons.

2. Cause and effect

Speeches arranged in causal order show a relationship between things or events. Causal speeches have two main points: one focusing on causes, the other on effects. The speaker attempts to show how the causes were instrumental in bringing about the effects.

3. Problem-solution

A problem-solution pattern begins by stating the problem or need and then offering a viable solution or remedy to it. The first main point illustrates the seriousness of the problem; the second main point proposes a solution to that problem.

4. Chronological

Chronological order follows a particular sequence: past, present, and future; first, second, and third; before and after. The sequence of steps is critical to the presentation. Reversing the order or mixing the sequence in any way undermines the purpose of the speech.

5. Spatial

Spatial organization works best if the presentation of a topic involves creating a visual picture based on location or direction. Speeches arranged spatially should

be accompanied by pictures, charts, videos, or other visual aids that show the size, location, shape, or direction being emphasized.
  B. Types of Configural Patterns
    1. Narrative
    Narrative speech patterns are organized as a story, complete with characters, plots, and drama. The audience must figure out the moral of the story or how it relates to the speech topic and occasion.
    2. Web
    In a web organizational pattern, speech ideas emanate from a central or core idea. The speaker begins by explaining the central idea and then explores the first idea. He or she brings it back to the central idea again by showing exactly how that point explains or extends the central purpose or idea. This process is repeated again and again.
    3. Problem-no solution
    With this organizational scheme, the problem is discussed at length, including its significance, but no solution is offered. The audience is encouraged to come up with solutions. This approach is particularly suitable for problems that require creative solutions.
    4. Multiple perspectives
    With this organizational structure, an idea or problem is analyzed from a variety of different viewpoints. The audience is exposed to alternative ways to look at an issue or to determine the best possible solution to a problem.
  C. Sample Speech Logics
    1. Linear organization
    The example in the text follows a typical problem-solution outline. With linear logic organization, each successive point advances the argument yet another step, culminating in a call for change or remedy to the growing problem. Main points are supported by rational facts. The speaker lays out the benefits for those willing to accept the proposed solution.
    2. Configural organization
    The example in the text follows the web pattern. With configural organization, the rationale for the problem is not defined directly; instead, the problem emerges indirectly through a pattern of stories, examples, and personal testimony that all come together to help the audience understand.

IV. Outlining
  A. Types of Outlines
  Complete sentence outlines consist of the entire introduction and conclusion written in full, all the main points and subpoints, examples and evidence, the purpose, and all the transitions that connect one idea to the next. Short phrase outlines are usually revised complete sentence outlines in which lengthy sentences are replaced with shorter phrases. Short phrase outlines can be used as notes for extemporaneous speaking.
  B. Simple Rules for Outlining Your Speech
    1. Every speech outline begins with a purpose statement specifying the speaker's intent and a thesis statement that lays out the central claim in the speech.
    2. Every outline consists of an introduction, a body, and a conclusion.
    3. The introduction consists of two parts: The attention-getter attracts audience interest in the topic; the preview provides an overview of the main points. Both parts should be written in paragraph form in the outline.
    4. The body of the speech consists of at least two main points indented and classified as I and II.

5. Main points from the body are followed by subpoints, indented again, and labeled with capital letters, A and B. Each main point must include at least two subpoints.
6. Sometimes subpoints are further subdivided into additional subdivisions—sub-subpoints, which are indented again and labeled with Arabic numbers (1 and 2). Anytime a subpoint can be subdivided, two sub-subpoints are required. These additional subdivisions generally refer to supporting materials.
7. The conclusion follows the body of the speech and consists of two parts: a summary and a memorable closing statement. The summary overviews the main points discussed in the body and the memorable closing statement finishes the presentation. The memorable statement should tie in the beginning comments with those at the end.
8. Every outline ends with a reference list. Reference lists contain only references used in the speech.

Classroom Exercises and Activities

1. Put students in groups of five to seven, assign all students in each group the same speech topic (e.g., gay and lesbian rights or legalization of marijuana). Have each group develop a brief outline of a speech on that topic using one type of linear logic. Then have representatives from each group share their outline with the rest of the class. Encourage the class to identify the specific linear pattern each group employed. Discuss how any speech topic can be organized in a variety of linear ways.

2. In extension of the first activity, have the same groups develop a speech outline on the same topic that relies on one of the configural speech patterns. Groups again share their organization with the class, which identifies the configural structure employed. Discuss how any speech topic can be organized in a variety of configural ways.

3. Videotape a conversation reflecting configural logic from a popular television show (e.g., "Friends," "Seinfeld," "Frasier") and show it to the class. Have students identify the type of logic employed in that conversation. Have students transform that same conversation into one of the linear patterns. Afterwards, ask students which logical structure made it easier to follow or understand. Which logical structure is more interesting or entertaining? Which logical structure do they prefer in everyday conversations? Which structure do they prefer for public speaking? Why?

4. Have students select five topics from the following list and generate a brief outline for each. Have them write a specific purpose statement, central thesis statement, and three main points and identify the organizational pattern they would use for each topic. After completing this project, select representative examples from each and show them to the class using the overhead projector. Discuss the variety of ways any given speech topic can be addressed.

   Protecting endangered species

   Being an organ donor

   How to make your own beef jerky

   Balancing the federal budget

   Solving the homeless problem

   Funding AIDS research

   Responsible pet ownership

   Three well-known exercise programs

   Subliminal advertising

   Vivisection

Weekend vacation trips

Federal regulation of child-care facilities

5. For every major speech, have students turn in a full-content outline as well as an abbreviated outline on notecards one week before the actual presentation. Give students feedback on both outlines.

6. Have students select one of the three speeches in the appendix and provide an appropriate outline. Follow up with these questions: Does the outline help you understand the speech any better? Did the speaker omit any supporting material that would have enhanced the quality of the speech? Could this speech have been organized another way? In what ways? What would you have done differently to make this outline better? Why? (See Part 5 in this manual for an analysis of the three speeches.)

7. After watching one of the three student speeches in the video that accompanies this text, have students write and turn in an abbreviated outline that the student speaker may have used to present that speech. Do this activity first with the linear informative speech (David Brashear) and then with the configural informative speech (Therese Rincon). Have students compare outlines for organizational format. (See Part 5 in this manual for the actual outlines employed for those speeches.) (This activity can be duplicated later on when persuasive speeches are assigned.)

Recommended Readings

Anderson, J. W. (1991). A comparison of Arab and American conceptions of "effective" persuasion. In L. A. Samovar & R. E. Porter (eds.), *Intercultural communication: A reader* (pp. 96–106). Belmont, CA: Wadsworth.

Anderson gives an excellent example of a comparative analysis of the rhetorical devices and strategies used in two advocacy advertisements created for the government of Saudi Arabia and Mobil Oil Corporation. As Anderson maintains, the two paid editorials "employ radically different rhetorical tactics to accomplish similar objectives" (p. 97). The reader is exposed to the types of arguments that characterize each culture.

Foss, S. K. (1989). *Rhetorical criticism: Exploration and practice*. Prospect Heights, IL: Waveland.

This book offers an overview of rhetorical criticism, including methods for understanding and practicing critical analysis. Chapter 5 provides an excellent introduction to feminist criticism, including examples of feminist criticisms of two different kinds of rhetorical artifacts from the point of view of women.

Kaplan, R. B. (1987). Cultural thought patterns revisited. In U. Connor and R. B. Kaplan (eds.), *Writing across languages: Analysis of L2 text* (pp. 9–21). Reading, MA: Addison-Wesley.

Kaplan argues that contrastive rhetoric characterizes essays written by those for whom English is a second language based on an analysis of written messages. He further argues that spoken language differs from written language. Nevertheless, communication scholars have extended Kaplan's claims to include the logics of orators. Is this a valid claim?

Tannen, D. T. (1990). *You just don't understand: Women and men in conversation*. New York: William Morrow.

Women and men often have trouble communicating with one another. According to Tannen, men are likely to value and use "logic" (read "linear logic") whereas women are likely to value and use "emotion" (read "contrastive logic"). Males' logic requires them to gather information, conduct surveys, and devise arguments as a researcher would do. Women rely on personal experience and making connections from the experiences of others. Men follow an argument step-by-step until it's settled; women often change course and seemingly digress. Apparently, the linear logic of Euroamericans represents more of a.male preference than a female preference, an idea worth investigating. (See especially pp. 91–93.)

CHAPTER 11

INTRODUCTIONS AND CONCLUSIONS

Learning Objectives

After studying the chapter, the student should be able to:

- Explain the primary three objectives of every introduction to a speech—to establish credibility, compel the audience to listen, and preview the speech.

- Explain what it means to "tell them what you just told them" when concluding a speech.

- Discuss the idea of leaving the audience wanting more when concluding a speech.

- Identify and give examples of each of the eight strategies to grab the audience's attention in introductions.

- Identify and give examples of each of the eight strategies used to arouse or motivate the audience in conclusions.

- Explain why she or he might want to avoid using clichés, disclaimers, and some rhetorical questions in introductions and conclusions.

Extended Chapter Outline

This chapter focuses on the properties of effective introductions and conclusions.

I. Beginning Your Speech
    A. Establish Your Credibility
       The audience should be provided with an introduction from a reliable source. The speaker should provide the audience with the specific qualifications or expertise he or she has regarding the topic. Attire and nonverbal communication are the first things the audience uses to judge the speaker. Looking composed is critical to appearing so.
    B. Compel Your Audience to Listen
       Speakers must compel the audience to listen by furnishing them with audience-centered reasons for listening. The more personal and audience-related are the reasons for listening, the more likely the audience will accept them. Beginning with a dramatic device, such as a humorous story, startling statement, or little-known fact will also motivate the audience to listen.
    C. Preview Your Speech: Tell Them What You're Going to Tell Them
       A preview gives an overview of the main points and helps the audience organize what's to come in a systematic way. The preview always comes at the end of the introduction.

II. Ending Your Speech
    A. Summarize Your Speech: Tell Them What You Just Told Them
        The summary provides the audience with a quick review of all major points. The summary immediately follows the discussion of the final point.
    B. Leave Them Wanting to Hear More
        The speaker should conclude with a dramatic or "gee-whiz!" ending. Ending remarks should hook up with opening remarks in a clever way, relying on a famous, relevant quotation or relating a dramatic story.

III. Strategies to Grab and Motivate Your Audience
    A. Personal Stories
        Beginning the speech with a personal story allows the audience to feel a sense of shared background, experience, and history. Ending the speech with a personal story helps bring home a point in the conclusion.
    B. Emotional Appeals
        Depending on the topic and the purpose of the presentation, the speaker may want to incite fear, guilt, anger, passion, pity, love, or other emotional responses. Emotional responses should not alienate the audience, but help form a common bond or empathy. Emotionally charged appeals are also effective in concluding remarks and are often effective in exciting the audience to take an action.
    C. Humor
        To be effective in an introduction or conclusion, humor must be funny and directly relevant to the point.
    D. Repetition
        Repetition—the repeated use of a word or phrase—adds rhythm to a speech and draws attention to the subject.
    E. Famous Quotations
        Famous, but familiar, quotes and the words of famous speakers, politicians, and entertainers are effective ways to begin or end a presentation. The originator of any quotation must be acknowledged during the speech.
    F. Startling Facts and Statistics
        Facts and statistics that amaze can entice the audience to listen or to leave with a "gee-whiz!" response.
    E. Dramatic Illustrations
        Beginning or concluding a presentation with a dramatic illustration or a story that paints a picture is an excellent rhetorical strategy. The more visual the experience, the more likely the audience will respond and remember it.

IV. Strategies to Avoid
    A. Overused Clichés
        Clichés are trite phrases or expressions that are common and overused. At one time, these phrases were effective, but due to overuse audiences view them as tiresome, unoriginal, and annoying.
    B. Disclaimers and Apologies
        Disclaimers are used to deny any responsibility for a faulty presentation. Apologies allow the speaker to assume total responsibility for doing a bad job or for having nothing further to contribute. Both are used to set up the audience for a failed presentation.
    C. Rhetorical Questions
        Rhetorical questions are those questions the speaker asks the audience without intending the audience to answer because he or she plans to answer them. Rhetorical questions can be effective at motivating the audience to listen, but if the questions are overused or trite, the speaker may appear tentative and lacking in conviction. Rhetorical questions can be turned into assertive declarative statements for more powerful results.

Classroom Exercises and Activities

1. Have groups of students read one of the assigned speeches in the appendix. Then ask each group to write their own introduction and conclusion to that speech. How do these introductions and conclusions differ from the original? How are theirs better? What strategies did they use to improve on the original?

2. Send students to the library to copy the introductions and conclusions from five different speeches of their choice from *Vital Speeches of the Day*; they should bring the copies to class. As a class, discuss how each are effective or ineffective. Discuss how they might be made better (rely on strategies discussed in the chapter). How does the occasion or setting influence the strategies a speaker uses to introduce (or conclude) a speech?

3. For their next speaking assignment, have students write three different introductions using three different strategies (e.g., personal story, emotional appeal, humor, and so on).

4. For their next speaking assignment, have students write three different conclusions, each using a different strategy (e.g., personal story, emotional appeal, humor, and so on).

5. Students often avoid selecting a famous quotation or a startling fact or statistic to introduce or conclude a speech. To give them practice with these techniques, you could require them to do so in their next formal speaking presentation.

6. Provide students with a hatful of speech topics from which to select one for an impromptu presentation. Allowing all students 2 minutes of preparation time, have one half of the students give a brief introduction and the other half a brief conclusion. Discuss strategies they can use to effectively accomplish either task.

Recommended Readings

Norton, R. (1983). *Communicator style: Theory, applications, and measures.* Beverly Hills, CA: Sage.

Bob Norton examines individuals' unique communicator styles; that is, the way one verbally or nonverbally signals how literal meaning should be interpreted or understood (p. 11). Of particular interest to our chapter, Norton offers a detailed profile of the dramatic communicator style (pp. 129–153). Dramatic communicators, according to Norton, "are especially effective because they capture our attention through their various devices, gimmicks, and tricks. In many instances, the attention-getting maneuvers are transparent, but in many more instances the attention-getting moves are seductive, charming, and compelling" (p. 129).

Fuller, E. (ed.). (1980). *2500 anecdotes for all occasions.* New York: Avenel Books.

This collection of anecdotes can be extremely useful to those searching for just the right opening or closing to a speech. Anecdotes are stories or parables that make a point or have a moral to relate. Some of these tales are famous; others are not. The anecdotes range from personality traits, business, sports, and religion to war, marriage, health, and justice.

Bartlett, J. (1992). *Familiar quotations.* Boston: Little, Brown.

This book is a standby. We have used it over and over again in our search for just the right quotation to use in a speech or an essay. You, too, will find it an invaluable resource. An author index and a subject index both help in searches for famous or familiar quotations.

American Heritage Dictionary (eds.) (1986). *Word mysteries and histories: From quiche to humble pie*. Boston: Houghton Mifflin.

This resource can be useful in the search for a clever introduction or conclusion. It's also an interesting book for those who enjoy words. For instance, did you know that "female" was originally unrelated to the word "male"? "Female" is a respelling of "femelle." Did you know what we call Democrats today were once called Republicans? These and other interesting word facts can provide you with the opportunity to astonish and engage your audience in unusual ways.

CHAPTER 12

INFORMING DIVERSE AUDIENCES: SPEAKING TO INFORM

Learning Objectives

After studying the chapter, the student should be able to:

- Define informative public speaking.
- List and explain the three goals of informative speaking.
- Differentiate between informative and persuasive public speaking.
- Identify the four types of informative speeches.
- Differentiate among the four types of informative speeches.
- Explain the differences between nontechnical and technical training presentations.
- Describe the basic format of an informative speech.
- Organize and outline an informative speech.
- List and discuss the six strategies to help make a speech easily understood by an audience.
- Distinguish between repetition and redundancy in a speech.
- Differentiate between transitions and signposts.
- Explain how three of the six strategies can be used effectively with particular co-cultural groups.
- Incorporate the six strategies into an effective informative speech.

Extended Chapter Outline

This chapter focuses on the goals, types, and organization of informative speeches.

I. Speaking to Inform
   An informative speech is a public presentation designed to change the way an audience thinks about a topic or an issue. The difference between informative and persuasive speeches is clear: informing teaches; persuading advocates.
   A. Goals of Informative Speaking
      1. Communicating new and unfamiliar information
         Informative speakers structure their speeches to introduce information to audiences about new and different topics.
      2. Extending what the audience already knows
         Informative speakers sometimes structure their speeches to extend the understanding and knowledge of audiences by communicating additional information about subjects that audience members already have some knowledge.

3. Updating old information
Informative speakers can bring new perspectives to an audience by reinterpreting or updating what an audience knows and believes about a subject. They attempt to correct misconceptions or reveal the latest research that alters what the audience might already believe to be true.

B. Types of Informative Speeches
1. Briefings and reports
A briefing or report presents recently available information to an audience that already has a general understanding of the topic.

2. Lectures
A lecture typically provides new or additional information about a particular subject; audience members are usually referred to as students. Good lectures often inform and entertain. Lectures are often more flexible and less tightly organized than other types of informative speeches.

3. Demonstrations
A demonstration is a short how-to speech explaining how to do a particular activity or use a specific object.

4. Training presentations
A training presentation teaches listeners to understand a concept or how to complete a task with an acceptable degree of accuracy. Training almost always involves adult learners who are required to attend and learn from the demonstration.
a. In nontechnical training presentations, a trainer, teacher, or instructor presents information to employees in a workplace environment that is set up exclusively for people to learn.
b. Technical training presentations teach an employee how to perform a particular, observable task with a given level of competence. Once an individual has been trained, the assumption is that he or she should be able to perform the task and will be evaluated in terms of quality or speed of performance.

II. Organizing and Outlining an Informative Speech
A. A Basic Format for Informing
All informative speeches have an identifiable introduction, body, and conclusion.
1. Introduction
The introduction should compel the audience to listen with an attention-getter and provide a preview of what's to come. The preview usually includes the thesis statement and an overview of the main points.

2. Body
Most informative speeches should contain no more than three main points, organized in a way that helps the audience make sense of the message. Once the main points and organizational pattern are set, identify what evidence supports which main point and place these subpoints in the correct location.

3. Conclusion
All informative speeches should include a brief summary of the main points. No new information should be given to the audience in the conclusion. An effective conclusion gives the audience a jolt and leaves them thinking about the speaker's message.

B. Outlining the Informative Speech
A detailed outline is mandatory and should include the following sections: title, specific purpose statement, thesis statement, introduction, body, conclusion, and references.

III. Strategies for Increasing Informational Effectiveness
  A. Keep It Simple
     The fewer points the speech presents, the more likely the audience will learn them. Too many numbers or statistics bore the audience. All definitions should be relatively brief and easy to understand.
  B. Keep It Concrete
     Avoid abstract explanations. The more abstract the issues and the more theoretical the explanations, the less likely the audience will comprehend the message. Use an everyday example to explain difficult concepts.
  C. Be Repetitive and Redundant
     Repetition refers to explaining something exactly the same way over and over again; it is essential for lists of simple, but important, concepts. Redundancy involves explaining something more than once, but in a slightly different way each time; it helps the audience remember more complex ideas and arguments. Without repetition and redundancy, the audience may fail to understand or simply miss key issues and explanations. Both strategies are especially important when speaking to audiences who communicate in English as their second or third language. Both repetition and redundancy increase the chances that understanding or comprehension will occur.
  D. Elicit Active Responses
     Stimulating the audience to do something in an open and public way increases understanding and retention. Eliciting an active audience response requires more than just asking the audience a question—the audience must be encouraged to respond. Dramatic nonverbal gestures are effective in encouraging audience response. Active audience response may be more natural for some co-cultures, such as African Americans, and less likely to occur in more collectivistic co-cultures, such as Asian and Native Americans.
  E. Use Familiar and Relevant Examples
     The speaker can help the audience to understand an unfamiliar idea by providing the audience with familiar and relevant examples that more simply illustrate the point. This strategy works well with audiences made up of individuals from diverse co-cultures. The challenge for the speaker is to find examples that are familiar and meaningful to other co-cultural audience members.
  F. Use Transitions and Signposts
     Transitions are statements or phrases that link together prior issues or points with the next ones. Signposts are simple words or phrases that signal organization. Both alert the audience to change or movement from one part of the speech to another. Transitions and signposts help the audience to visualize the speech outline and to follow the presentation with little or no effort. Both strategies are effective with audiences of all co-cultures.

Classroom Exercises and Activities

1. Show the class the two videotaped informative speeches that accompany this text (David Brashear and Therese Rincon, "The Coffee House Craze"). Have them discuss what they liked about each speech. Why was each speaker effective? What constituted the introduction, body, and conclusion of each speech? What specific strategies did David and Therese use to increase informational effectiveness? (Keep it simple, keep it concrete, be repetitive and redundant, and so on.)

2. Invite a particularly effective math or science teacher to talk to the class about strategies she or he uses to make complex information simple and interesting to a potentially disinterested group of students. Someone from the medical community might discuss ways to simplify complex medical information for a lay audience.

3. Select a particularly difficult passage from a textbook or research journal. Copy it for the entire class. Have students write a passage translating what the author says. Afterwards, have students identify what strategies they used to make the information more palatable or acceptable.

4. To show the pervasiveness of informative speaking, have students generate a list of individuals that regularly make informative presentations as a part of their profession. Also, list those events or occasions that generally require an informative presentation of some kind.

Recommended Readings

Beighley, K. C. (1952). A summary of experimental studies dealing with the effect of organization and of skill of speaker on comprehension, *Journal of Communication, 2,* 58–65.

This research report describes a six-study investigation into the influence of organized and disorganized written material on reader retention. All six studies support the conclusion that organized materials produce more receiver retention than disorganized materials. This early investigation provides good insight into the importance of effective organization in speech preparation.

Katzer, J., Cook, K. H., & Crouch, W. W. (1982). *Evaluating information: A guide for users of social science research* (2nd ed.). Reading, MA: Addison-Wesley.

This excellent book about the nature of information is a valuable resource for speakers who are assembling data for an informative presentation. The authors discuss how we come to know what we know, the discovery process, the interpretation of information, the kinds of information that are believable, and how to evaluate the quality of information.

Kemp, J. E. (1985). Teaching/learning activities. In J. E. Kemp, *The instructional design process* (pp. 99–130). New York: Harper & Row.

This chapter adds insight to our discussion on training and instructional presentations. The author describes the patterns of effective classroom presentation, the conditions that lead to receiver comprehension and learning, and the elements of establishing relationships between instructors (informative speakers) and learners (audience members).

Hamilton, C., & Parker, C. (1990). Informative presentations. In C. Hamilton & C. Parker, *Communicating for results: A guide for business and the professions* (3rd ed.) (pp. 315–348). Belmont, CA: Wadsworth.

This chapter discusses some of the same material in Chapter 12 but from a business-oriented perspective. The authors develop an interesting distinction between formal and informal informative presentations. There is also a meaningful discussion on strategies for successfully informing different types of audiences.

Seiler, W. F., Baudhuim, E. S., & Schuelke, L. D. (1982). Information acquisition and transfer in organizations. In W. F. Seiler, E. S. Baudhuim, & L. D. Schuelke, *Communication in business and professional organizations* (pp. 152–169). Reading, MA: Addison-Wesley.

This is a chapter on the process of informing more generally. The authors define information, distinguish the types of information, discuss misconceptions about information, and explain a number of strategies for increasing the effectiveness of information. The material is discussed within the context of the organization.

CHAPTER 13

PERSUADING DIVERSE AUDIENCES: SPEAKING TO PERSUADE

Learning Objectives

After studying the chapter, the student should be able to:

- List and differentiate among the three goals of persuasive speaking.
- Define and discuss the five types of persuasive speeches.
- Explain the human tendency to resist change.
- Discuss ways to adapt to an audience that already agrees with one's position.
- Discuss ways to adapt to an audience that already disagrees with one's position.
- Discuss ways to adapt to an audience that is neutral to or undecided about one's position.
- Explain why the organization of a persuasive speech plays such a central role in achieving change.
- List and describe the five steps of Monroe's Motivated Sequence.
- Organize and outline a persuasive speech using the five steps of Monroe's Motivated Sequence.
- List and explain the nine strategies for persuading audiences.
- Explain the ethical implications of using fear appeals in a persuasive speech.
- Incorporate the nine strategies into a presentation that will manage potential audience resistance to a persuasive speech.

Extended Chapter Outline

This chapter focuses on the goals, types, and organization of an effective persuasive speech for diverse audiences.

I. Speaking to Persuade
   The goal of a persuasive speech is to advocate. The speaker wants the audience to feel, think, or behave differently than it did before the speech.
   A. Changing Attitudes
      The speaker intends to move the audience in such a way that members feel more positively or negatively as a result of the speech. The predetermined goal is to change the audience's feelings or emotions.

B. Changing Beliefs
Beliefs refer to the perception of the truth or falsity of a given proposition. Persuading the audience to change beliefs about an issue or idea can be very similar to informative speaking — adding new information can often provoke individuals to rethink or reexamine everything they thought to be true or false. Persuasion occurs when the audience becomes convinced that an idea once thought to be true (or false) is now seen as false (or true). To accomplish persuasion, the speaker must both inform the audience (add new information that conflicts with what was thought to be true) and advocate the acceptance of a new belief.

C. Changing Behavior
The goal of all persuasive speaking is to change audience behavior, which requires that the speaker motivate the audience into taking or committing to some kind of action. Persuasive speeches that emphasize behavior change focus more on explicit behavioral outcomes than persuasive speeches that emphasize either attitude or belief changes.

D. Types of Persuasive Speeches
1. Political speeches
Political speeches are meant to change or reinforce audience beliefs on a political issue or to secure votes at the polls. Compared to other kinds of persuasive speech types, political speeches are highly crafted, thoroughly tested, and well rehearsed.

2. Speeches advocating social change
Speeches advocating social change tell audience members how they should feel, think, or behave and emphasize behavioral change.

3. Sermons
The primary goal of most sermons or religious presentations is inspirational. The persuasive message is designed to change or reinforce the audience's attitudes toward God or some other supreme being or beings. Beliefs are probed and moral behaviors advocated.

4. Motivational speeches
Motivational speeches are designed to persuade audience members to feel better about themselves and do something about their lives. The primary goal of a motivational speech is attitude change accompanied by a behavior change that produces a positive outcome.

II. Considering the Audience
A. The Human Tendency to Resist Change
When audience members discover that the goal of a presentation is to change how they feel or what they think, they typically resist or rebel. Any attempt at controlling behavior is likely to be perceived as threatening to personal freedoms. To counteract this universal human inclination to resist change, speakers can focus on reasons why the audience must change, convince the audience that there's something wrong with the status quo, and use less direct methods to call for behavioral change.

B. Adapting to Your Audience
1. If the audience already agrees with the advocated position, the speaker should adjust the purpose of the speech to intensify audience attitudes, beliefs, and behaviors. Remind audience members of why they hold the shared attitudes toward the issue. Speakers should also provide motivation to intensify or strengthen audience members' attitudes by using emotional appeals. Speakers can be more direct or explicit with a supportive audience when calling for them to change.

2. With a neutral or undecided audience, the speaker must get members sufficiently interested to listen before persuasion can occur. He or she should provide some unbiased background on the controversy, reveal personal attitudes and beliefs about the issue, and support a position with evidence.

3. When an audience disagrees with the speaker, only a slight change in attitude can be expected. The speaker should plan on moving the audience from complete disagreement to less disagreement. She or he should show the audience that the opposing position is understood and appreciated, highlight areas of disagreement, set aside areas of disagreement that need not be dealt with during this speech, and back her or his position with credible evidence.

III. Organizing and Outlining a Persuasive Speech

Organization plays a central role in a persuasive speech: The logic used must establish why the audience must change. (Unless audience members feel that there is something wrong with what they are doing or feeling, they are unlikely to change.) While Monroe's Motivated Sequence is the most widely used organizational pattern for persuasive speaking, the cause-and-effect, problem-solution, narrative, web, and multiple-perspective techniques are also effective in preempting psychological resistance to change.

A. Monroe's Motivated Sequence
   1. Gain the audience's attention
      Attention-getters grab the audience, arousing curiosity about what the speaker is going to say. To help avoid the effects of psychological reactance, the preview statement should be omitted.
   2. Identify unfulfilled needs
      The speaker must establish clear, urgent, and unfilled needs in the minds of the audience. This is a critical step in the sequence. No solutions should be proposed during this stage.
   3. Propose a solution that satisfies those needs
      Present the solution to the needs or problems described in step two. During this stage, speakers must also identify and eliminate possible objections to the solution.
   4. Visualize what satisfaction will mean
      Intensify audience members' desire for the solution by getting them to visualize what their lives will be like once they've adopted it. Use vivid images and verbal illustrations to support the benefits of the proposed solution.
   5. Define specific actions
      In the final step, the speaker must turn the audience's agreement and commitment into a positive action. Tell audience members what they need to do to obtain the described solution and its benefits.

B. Making the Most of Monroe's Motivated Sequence
   To make the most of Monroe's Motivated Sequence, the steps should be followed in sequence. The sequence most closely resembles a problem-solution organizational format, but digresses from linear logic in several ways. In the attention step, the purpose statement and preview are omitted. During the satisfaction step, the structure tends to deviate from linearity by noting potential objections and dispelling audience concerns or problems with a solution. In the forth step, visualization is inserted in an otherwise predominantly linear sequence. The most critical principle in Monroe's sequence is the identification of the audience's needs before proposing a solution.

C. Outlining a Persuasive Speech
   Each of the five steps in Monroe's Motivated Sequence should be represented by a Roman numeral. Main points and subpoints are represented by capital letters and numbers respectively. (See Chapter 10 for more on outlining.)

IV. Nine Strategies for Persuading
   A. Conceal the Intent to Persuade
      Because people are naturally predisposed to resist change, this strategy allows the speaker to wait until identifying an audience need before revealing a solution.

Revealing the purpose of the speech too early can trigger psychological reactance; concealing it altogether can compromise speaker ethics.

B. Don't Ask for Too Much

The speaker's message should not demand more than what is realistic in the way of change. When demanding a complete change in audience attitude or behavior, the speaker promotes psychological reactance and risks the boomerang effect, in which the outcome is opposite what the persuader wanted to achieve. A more effective approach is to ask for small incremental changes.

C. Avoid Inflammatory Phrases

Unfortunate phrases can backfire. Select words and phrases carefully so they do not arouse negative feelings.

D. Use a Two-Sided Message with Refutation

One-sided messages give only the speaker's side the argument. Two-sided messages attempt to give both sides a fair hearing. Two-sided messages with refutation present both sides and refute or deny the validity or worth of the opposing side. Audiences are most influenced when the speaker uses two-sided messages with refutation.

E. Inoculate against Counterarguments

When a speaker is preceded or followed by another who advocates a contrary position, a two-sided message with refutation becomes essential. This strategy is helpful when the speaker knows that the audience already agrees with his or her position, but wants to ensure the audience isn't swayed by the other speaker. Consequently, the speaker inoculates or immunizes the audience against counterpropaganda by systematically destroying what the other speaker is likely to say or has already said. Evidence plays an important role in the inoculation process.

F. Keep Objections to a Minimum

The number of audience objections dealt with and the time spent on them should be limited. Only a couple of objections should be raised. Since the purpose of the speech is to persuade the audience in the opposite direction of the objections, too much attention to objections could expose the audience to the opposite position to too large an extent.

G. Combine Reason with Emotion

Evidence such as facts, statistics, and physical data should be included in any persuasive speech. In spite of co-cultural preferences, however, all groups respond to emotional appeals. Emotional appeals are likely to motivate an audience to do something or to take an action. Speakers who use emotional appeals have the responsibility to use it for only ethical purposes.

H. Use Fear Appeals—When Appropriate

Recent research indicates that strong fear appeals persuade an audience to change an attitude or behavior. Fear appeals should only be used when they are appropriate to the topic, however. The decision to use high fear as a persuasive technique must take into account the ethics involved in scaring people: An ethical speaker behaves responsibly and tells the truth when using fear to persuade; an unethical speaker distorts information and deceives the audience with fear.

I. Repeat Your Message

Repeat main points to increase audience attention and retention. With repetitions, audience members are more likely to recall the arguments more accurately, understand the message more thoroughly, and become more convinced of the proposed solution. Messages that are repeated too often, however, are likely to provoke reactance, irritation, or boredom. A point should not be repeated more than three times.

Classroom Exercises and Activities

1. Show the class the videotaped persuasive speech that accompanies this text ("Powering Ourselves" by Tamara Synigal). Have them discuss what they liked about her speech. Why was Tamara effective? What constituted the attention, need, satisfaction (solution), visualization, and action steps of her speech? What specific strategies did Tamara use to persuade her audience? (Keep objections to a minimum, combine reason with emotion, and so on.)

2. Have students view Tamara's videotaped speech several times. Ask them to write an abbreviated outline. Then, compare their outlines to the one Tamara wrote (see Part 5 of this manual for her outline). Discuss how to organize and outline a persuasive speech using Monroe's Motivated Sequence.

3. Have students outline the persuasive speeches presented in the appendix of their text: "Television Can Be Murder" by Mehdi Safaie and "Take a Stand for Human Rights" by Charles Park. Discuss ways both speakers might have improved their persuasive speeches. How could they have better developed the need step? The action step? What specific strategies did Mehdi and Charles use to persuade their audience? What other strategies could they have used?

4. Ask students to watch or videotape several television commercials or bring in several videotaped commercials yourself. Ask them to identify the five steps of Monroe's Motivated Sequence used in each commercial. Which steps appeared to be emphasized or deemphasized? Why? What recommendations would you give to advertisers of those commercials?

5. Have students (in groups) select three items from the following list of thesis statements and design appropriate fear appeals for each. Then have them design a concrete, feasible, and effective way for the audience to reduce their fear.

   Don't use drugs.

   The sun is hazardous to your health.

   Grades are important.

   Television violence has become far too explicit.

   Teachers should not date their students.

   There is no such thing as "safe sex."

   Guns don't kill; people do.

   Using credit cards can be disastrous.

   Have students share their fear appeals and solutions with the class. Discuss the ethics associated with using fear as a persuasive appeal.

6. Ask students to select a controversial topic such as right to life, gun control, use of contraceptives by teenagers, social welfare programs, term limits, and so on. For the topic they select, ask them to present orally or in writing a two-sided message with refutation designed to persuade others to their point of view. Encourage class members to evaluate whether both sides were presented fairly.

   A variation on this activity is to have students identify their own position on a controversial topic and then create an argument that supports the side they disagree with. Afterward, talk about how counterattitudinal advocacy really works!

Recommended Readings

Ajzen, I. (1988). *Attitudes, personality, and behavior*. Chicago: Dorsey Press.

This text provides an excellent discussion of the relationship between attitudes and behavior. When and how does attitude change influence how we behave? Can engaging in a new behavior simultaneously influence a change in attitude? The author explains how attitudes and personality characteristics influence what an individual actually does in a variety of social situations. This book will be particularly helpful to the students interested in preparing speeches that influence behaviors as opposed to attitudes alone.

Boster, F., & Mongeau, P. (1984). Fear arousing persuasive messages. In R. Bostrom (ed.), *Communication yearbook 8* (pp. 330–377). Beverly Hills, CA: Sage.

This article reviews all the relevant research on fear appeals in persuasion. Boster and Mongeau also provide a metaanalysis of that research. Their results indicate that high, not moderate or low, fear appeals are most effective at influencing attitude or behavior change. Unfortunately, most introductory textbooks in our field continue to misinform by relying on the results of a single study published forty years ago. Boster and Mongeau set the record straight.

Reardon, K. K. (1991). *Persuasion in practice* (2nd ed.). Newbury Park, CA: Sage.

This text provides an excellent, up-to-date overview of the theory and research on persuasion. A number of important theories are discussed, including those referenced in our chapter here, which will help you understand why and how attempts to influence are effective or not.

Zimbardo, P. G., & Leippe, M. R. (1991). *The psychology of attitude change and social influence*. New York: McGraw Hill.

This text, a revised edition of an earlier text by Zimbardo, provides the undergraduate with a solid understanding of the research and thinking on communication and social influence. The authors also effectively discuss the current thinking on persuasion in a variety of applied contexts, including legal and health care settings.

CHAPTER 14

VERBAL COMMUNICATION: MAKING EVERY WORD COUNT

Learning Objectives

After studying the chapter, the student should be able to:

- Explain why it is critically important to make every word count when preparing and delivering a speech.

- List and explain the six strategies that help the audience better understand a message.

- Discuss the kinds of attributions audiences make about speakers who communicate with noticeable accents and dialects.

- Explain what speakers with an accent or a dialect should do to increase audience receptivity to them.

- Discuss strategies that will help make the English as a second language (ESL) speaker better understood by an audience.

- Describe how using the imaginative imagery of language can help make a message come across as powerful and strong.

- Differentiate among the images that can be created using concrete images, similes, and metaphors.

- Discuss the advantages of using intense, animated language in a speech.

- Explain the advantages of using active rather than passive voice in a speech.

- Understand how bias-free language includes, rather than alienates, an audience.

- Define the concept of verbal immediacy.

- Explain how being verbally immediate as a speaker can stimulate feelings of closeness and inclusion in a audience.

- Describe speaker strategies that help the audience notice and remember what the speaker had to say.

Extended Chapter Outline

This chapter focuses on the verbal communication strategies necessary for an effective presentation.

I. Speak to Be Understood
  A. Keep It Simple
    Using simple, clear, concise language helps the audience focus on the core issues of the speaker's argument. Simple words can replace or complement sophisticated, complex thoughts.

B. Limit Your Use of Jargon and Acronyms
Define specialized jargon and acronyms for the audience. Use professional jargon sparingly.

C. Avoid Phrases That Don't Say Anything
Avoid using bloated speech or words and sentences that say nothing or are intended to be ambiguous. Comments or lines that contribute nothing to the meaning of the speech can reduce speaker credibility and confuse the audience.

D. Pronounce Your Words Accurately
Speaker credibility suffers when audience members catch a speaker mispronouncing words or names.

E. Adapt to Audience Responses to Your Accent or Dialect
Regional, racial, and ethnic dialects and accents bring with them positive and negative attributions about the speaker's level of intelligence, social status, credibility, and power. Dialect refers to the different words or labels people use for the same phenomenon. Accent refers to the way words are said or pronounced. To ensure that the message is clearly understood, speakers should:
1. Check to make sure the audience understands the particular words and phrases being used by regularly looking for nonverbal cues and actively eliciting their feedback.
2. Clarify or translate the meanings of words and phrases.
3. Recognize and respect the audience's unique dialect and accent and occasionally use one of the words or phrases unique to their region or co-culture.

F. Appreciate Your Efforts to Speak English as a Second Language
The following are some strategies to help make the English as a second language (ESL) speaker better understood:
1. Speak a little slowly so that audience members can adjust to slight differences in the speech.
2. Use gestures and facial expressions to reinforce the meaning of the speech.
3. Do not apologize for any difficulties with the language.
4. Use, and translate for the audience, words and phrases from his or her primary language.

II. Speak to Show Strength
A. Use Imaginative Imagery
Imagery involves the use of carefully chosen words and phrases that appeal to the senses of touch, taste, sound, sight, and smell.
1. Concrete images
Vivid images are most easily aroused with the use of concrete language. Such images help the audience attend to and perceive the message with greater enthusiasm and accuracy than more abstract messages.
2. Similes
Similes create images through the use of an expressed analogy. Similes show a direct comparison by using the word "like" or "as" (i.e., "slept like a baby" and "dumb as a board").
3. Metaphors
Metaphors develop a picture by implied analogy. Metaphors compare an object to another object (i.e., "can't see the forest for the trees").

B. Use Intense, Animated Language
Vivid language contributes to attitude and behavioral change. Substitute dramatic words for drab ones; use action words; employ similes and metaphors; and offer more descriptive detail. Intense, animated language makes the presentation more gripping and appealing.

C. Choose the Active Voice
   Substitute passive words with active words to inject vigor and vitality into the speech. Make the subject of the sentence perform.
D. Use Power Words and Avoid Unnecessary Qualifiers
   By eliminating qualifying phrases (i.e., the "I'm not sure" in "I'm not sure, but he looks sick to me") from the speech, the speaker is perceived as stronger, more assertive, and factual.

III. Speak to Include, Not Alienate
   A. Use Bias-Free Language
      To be effective in a culturally diverse society, speakers must avoid reinforcing questionable attitudes and assumptions about people's ethnicity, gender, or other co-cultural affiliation.
      1. Apply the principle of self-definition
         One of the most important guidelines for speaking inclusively is to use names or labels that the individuals or groups listening to the speech choose for themselves.
      2. Don't mention group membership unnecessarily
         If a co-cultural affiliation (i.e., "a *female* prosecutor") is irrelevant to your point, don't bring it up.
      3. Give parallel treatment
         Parallel treatment requires that the speaker provide similar labels for comparable groups. "Man" and "woman" are parallel labels, as are "husband" and "wife." "Man" and "wife," however are nonparallel.
      4. Be inclusive and avoid making unwarranted assumptions
         Don't use wording that leaves out individuals or groups or that treats them as other than equals (i.e., "All law school graduates and their wives are invited to the picnic" assumes that all such graduates are male.)
      5. Avoid the use of masculine terms as generics
         Masculine pronouns should not be used as generic terms that refer to both women and men. There are a variety of remedies for eliminating this bias.
         a. Use the plural "they."
         b. Use the second person "you."
         c. Omit the pronoun.
         d. Pair the pronouns ("he or she").
         e. Rephrase the statement.
      6. Don't use feminine endings
         Feminine endings such as "-ess" and "-ette" specify gender when it's irrelevant, imply that the male is the norm, and carry the sense of smallness or cuteness. If the gender of the person is important to the speech, use adjectives or pronouns to indicate gender.
      7. Remember that people are people first
         Describing people by a particular characteristic may be inappropriate. Mention the person before giving any qualifiers, and don't mention the qualifier at all unless it's relevant to the speech.
      8. Watch for hidden bias
         A speaker can send a biased message even when biased terms are avoided. For example, "more unmarried women than ever before are having babies" is a biased statement; "more unmarried couples than ever before are having babies" is not.
   B. Practice Being Verbally Immediate
      Immediacy behaviors include word choices and language strategies that appear to reduce physical or psychological distance between the speaker and the audience. Immediacy behaviors stimulate feelings of closeness and inclusion. A useful strategy

to appear immediate to others is to use first-person pronouns such as "we" and "us" and avoid second- or third-person pronouns such as "you," "them," or "they."

    C. Avoid Profanity

Don't use profanity. Being profane is more than using coarse language; it's showing irreverence or contempt for something that others find sacred or meaningful.

IV. Speak to Be Noticed and Quoted

    A. Maintain Rhythm and Momentum

Rephrasing and restating key phrases and words helps build momentum and rhythm into a speech. Rephrasing with similar, redundant words or word series can add pulse or cadence to an otherwise ordinary presentation. Besides eliciting attention, rhythmic speech subtly stimulates the audience to focus, learn, and remember central ideas in the presentation.

    B. Use Humor

Humor includes jokes or funny, relevant short stories. When used appropriately, humor can disarm even the most hostile of audiences, making it more receptive or open to the speaker's message. Humor helps establish rapport with the audience.

    C. Create Your Own Sound Bites

Sound bites are brief passages taken from a press release or presentation to be reprinted or taped for later news reports. Speakers should create sound bites by planning and systematically selecting the right word or lines that capture the meaning and emotion of the message.

Classroom Exercises and Activities

1. As a class or in groups, students should brainstorm and list metaphors and similes they commonly use or have heard others use. Then ask them to create new metaphors and similes for every trite one they included on their initial list. Share them with the class. Discuss how metaphors and similes can be useful to a speaker.

2. Develop a list of words for your students (see below). The only criterion for your list is common usage. As an individual or class activity, ask students to substitute each common word with a more uncommon synonym that is more concrete, animated, or intense. To help get them started, try our list:

Rich	Tax increase
Said	Money
Building	Cheap
Cold	Tall
Wrong	Blue
Decrease	Hungry
Love	Sad
Asked	Nervous
Tired	Polite
Good	Fat
Bad	A *difficult* child
Ill	Spoiled
Poor	Angry

3. Chapter 14 includes the entire text of former First Lady Barbara Bush's commencement speech at Wellesley. Have students assume the role of a newspaper reporter covering the speech to college graduates and their families and respond to the following questions:

   a. What sound bites would you use in your newspaper coverage? List as many as you might use.

   b. What criteria did you use to determine your selection of sound bites?

   c. Of the sound bites you selected, which are best and why?

   d. What functions do sound bites serve?

   e. Do sound bites primarily distort or illuminate the facts?

4. Have students as a class develop a list of words that have caused personal confusion due to inconsistent denotative and connotative meanings (e.g., slang words such as "bad" or "gay"). You may want to extend this list to include words or labels that have negative meanings associated with them (e.g., "liberal" and "feminist"). How can these words be modified or relabeled to avoid negative meanings in the future?

5. Every co-culture has its own set of expressions. Have students identify expressions or phrases that are unique to their own co-cultural background. To get them started, provide the following list and have them trace their derivatives:

   "I'm busier than a cat covered up."

   "Way!"

   "Not."

   "It's raining cats and dogs."

   "Get a life."

   "Geez Louise."

   "Birds of a feather."

   "To die for."

   "He (or she) is a pistol."

   "Crocodile tears."

   "Get a hold" of somebody.

   "Weasel word."

   "Scaredy cat" or "Chicken."

   "Far out" or "Groovy."

   "Get down."

   "Dough" or "Bread"

   "Bro."

   "Crib."

   "Hood."

Recommended Readings

Fisher, H. (1981). *Improving voice and articulation* (3rd ed.). Boston, MA: Houghton Mifflin.

This is now the classic book in the field of voice and articulation. It clearly distinguishes between pronunciation and articulation in discussing the variety of speech and delivery problems that can be improved in the classroom. It includes guidelines for fixing speech problems such as running sounds and words together.

Payne, L. V. (1969). *The lively art of writing*. New York: Mentor.

Although written to help novice writers write better, this book has ideas suitable for constructing speeches as well. Chapters 8, 9, 10, and 11 are especially pertinent to the ideas and verbal strategies recommended in the textbook. Payne talks about converting sentences from passive to active voice, using metaphors and similes, and the importance of speech rhythm.

CHAPTER 15

NONVERBAL COMMUNICATION: MAKING EVERY GESTURE COUNT

Learning Objectives

After studying the chapter, the student should be able to:

- Define and discuss the concept of nonverbal communication.

- Discuss what it means to look like a public speaker.

- Choose and wear clothing that makes her or him look like a credible public speaker.

- Discuss how clothing is often used to communicate how a person feels or wants others to think he or she feels.

- Emphasize gestures that help a public presentation and eliminate those that can hurt it.

- Explain the relationship between looking composed as a speaker and making a good impression on an audience.

- Distinguish among nonverbal emblems, nonverbal adaptors, and nonverbal illustrators.

- Explain why it is important to make eye contact with every member of an audience.

- Maintain eye contact with an audience during speeches.

- Identify and employ nonverbal strategies that help keep the audience interested in what is being said.

- Vary voice for emphasis and to increase audience attention to important points in a speech.

- Explain how silence or pause time is an effective strategy to hold the audience's attention.

- Define and explain the concept of nonverbal immediacy.

- Employ nonverbal immediacy behaviors that initiate and maintain psychological closeness and warmth with the audience.

Extended Chapter Outline

This chapter focuses on the effects of nonverbal communication on a public presentation.

I. Look Like a Public Speaker
    Nonverbal communication can be defined as the intentional or unintentional use of our bodies to provoke or arouse meanings in others.
    A. Clothing Communicates Power and Status
       Power and status are commonly associated with how a person dresses. Although some speaking occasions are less formal and require less formal attire, most public speaking occasions require formal attire. Dressing professionally increases speaker credibility.
    B. Clothing Communicates How We Feel
       Clothing is often used to communicate how a person feels or wants others to think she or he feels. Specific clothing can be used to identify with the audience. Speakers should dress in a manner appropriate to the occasion and audience.

II. Use Your Body Effectively
    Looking composed is critical to impression formation. The gestures used during a presentation can either contribute to the impression of being relaxed and in control or undermine it.
    A. Nonverbal Emblems
       Emblems are nonverbal gestures that have direct verbal translations that are widely understood. Emblems can be substituted for words. Sometimes gestures can be vague or difficult to read for certain audience members. Unless the speaker is sure that everyone in the audience shares the same meaning for an emblem, they should not be used.
    B. Nonverbal Adaptors
       Adaptors are unintentional hand, arm, leg, or other body movements used to reduce stress or relieve boredom. When a speaker uses adaptors, such as pulling at a beard, smoothing the sleeve of a coat, or adjusting and readjusting eyeglasses, the audience assumes the speaker is nervous and unprepared. Uncontrolled use of adaptors can be a problem for the speaker.
    C. Nonverbal Illustrators
       Illustrators are hand and arm movements that demonstrate and reinforce the meanings intended by verbal messages. Illustrators can be helpful in communicating to the audience that a speaker is composed and in control. Illustrators help the speaker communicate the message by adding a kind of redundancy to the verbal message, and are intentionally used to help communicate meaning when words alone may not be adequate. Illustrators are exaggerated gestures that help ensure accuracy and understanding.

III. Look at Your Audience
    As soon as he or she reaches the podium, the speaker should make eye contact with every individual audience member. Smiling, nodding, holding eye contact for a moment, and saying hello are recognition strategies that acknowledge the audience. Eye contact acts as a powerful stimulus for eliciting audience involvement. The more speaker-audience eye contact there is, the more likely the audience will stay interested and attentive. Eye contact obligates audience members to do something in return. In the case of public speaking, audience response usually takes the form of head-nodding, smiling, and reciprocated eye contact.

IV. Keep Your Audience Interested
    Overall body movement is another way a speaker can make a difference in how attentive or bored she or he appears. A confident, purposeful stride presents an eager and energized speaker. Posture is also an important element that can be used to hold the

audience's interest. Leaning into the podium stresses an important point. Direct, face-to-face body posture also suggests active interaction and a sense of inclusion or belonging to the group.

V. Use Your Voice to Your Advantage
  A. Vary Vocal Volume and Pitch
     Change the volume. Speak softly when you want the audience to quiet down. Speak loudly, but gradually increase volume for effect. Dramatize a story by culminating the final lines in a loud, booming voice or by gradually decreasing volume to show the seriousness or gravity of the event. The point is, keep changing the volume.
  B. Vary Speech Rate
     Audiences prefer speakers to vary their speech rate (how fast or slow the speaker talks). Research indicates that faster rates of speech tend to increase, rather than decrease, listener comprehension and recall. Slow rates are effective during introductory and closing remarks, and when the audience may have trouble adjusting to accent or dialect. At other times, a normal speed or a faster rate of speech keeps the audience attentive and promotes recall.
  C. Use Silence Strategically
     Silence or pause time is an effective strategy to hold the audience's attention. A pregnant pause used before or after a phrase or line can add special meaning and emphasis to the message. Silence strategies include putting down notes, taking off glasses, moving closer to the audience, and scanning the audience. Pause time can go a long way toward capturing audience attention and building suspense and drama.

VI. Practice Being Nonverbally Immediate
   A speaker can establish a sense of closeness with the audience by the nonverbal behaviors used. Besides eye contact, smiling, the use of illustrators, forward leaning, and vocal variety, nonverbal immediacy behaviors also include head-nodding, open gestures, touch, and standing close to the audience. Immediacy behaviors show warmth, friendliness, and liking. Speakers who engage in behaviors that communicate immediacy are likely to get similar behaviors from the audience. This reciprocal behavior is consistent across all co-cultures. Strategies that promote nonverbal immediacy include:
   1. Moving away from the podium, table, or desk while communicating.
   2. Moving toward the audience and then away.
   3. Using postures or stances that are relaxed and comfortable.

Classroom Exercises and Activities

1. For each of the nonverbal emblems presented in Chapter 15 (see the highlighted box in the text), have students identify their verbal equivalent or meaning.

2. Divide the class into groups of five to seven people and hand each group an envelope containing seven slips of paper, each with one of the instructions below. Instruct students to look only at the slip of paper he or she draws from the envelope. Each student should then nonverbally signal or act out to the group the instructions listed on her or his slip of paper while students from the other groups name the meaning of each nonverbal signal.

   a. Nonverbally signal that you are bored and uninterested in what is going on in the group.

   b. Nonverbally signal that you want the floor or a chance to speak.

   c. Nonverbally signal that you are angry with the group members.

   d. Nonverbally signal to a particular group member (choose anyone you wish) that you find him or her attractive or interesting.

e. Indicate nonverbally that you are time conscious and want the group to hurry up with the assignment.

f. Ask a question for information in such a way that your vocal cues, facial expression, movements, and eyes all signal that you are in charge and want to be the boss.

g. You see one group member as a nuisance and a threat to your status. Indicate nonverbally how you might put her or him down by using nonverbal "one-up" signals.

3. We talk about time in a variety of ways: "time flies," "time won't wait," "time goes by," "time is money," and so on. Have students brainstorm in groups and make a list of all the different ways we talk about time. Afterward, ask students to examine their list carefully and answer the following questions as a class:

a. Given the large number of ways Americans talk about time, what does that communicate about our preoccupation with time (particularly with Euroamericans)?

b. Why is time so important to Euroamericans? Why is it relatively unimportant to some other co-cultures?

c. How do people abuse time? What happens to people when they abuse it?

d. Why is time important when giving a presentation? What happens to speakers who go way under or overtime?

4. Have students identify annoying nonverbal adaptors that speakers (and teachers) use. Then have students list the adaptors they themselves tend to use. What functions do such adaptors serve? Lead the class in a discussion to determine what they can do to manage or eliminate their use of annoying adaptors.

5. Ask a volunteer student to recite aloud the following line — "A frog jumped out of the water" — using vocal variations to express one of the emotions listed below. Have class members identify the expressed emotion. The student who correctly guesses the emotion then replaces the first speaker and recites the exact same line using another emotion. Repeat this exercise until all emotions are expressed and correctly guessed.

Anger	Reverence
Disgust	Relief
Love	Uncertainty
Hate	Surprise
Jealousy	Joy
Boredom	Pain
Passion	

Following this exercise, discuss the importance of vocal expressiveness in presenting a speech.

6. Have students describe the typical clothing or uniform they wear to look casual and to look dressed up and formal. Have them describe how their casual or formal look influences how they communicate, if at all. What effect does casual and formal clothing have on a speaker's presentation? On how the audience perceives her or him?

Recommended Readings

Burgoon, J. K., Buller, D. B., & Woodall, W. G. (1989). *Nonverbal communication: The unspoken dialogue*. New York: Harper & Row.

This well-written, fairly advanced textbook provides an update of all the relevant research done on nonverbal communication. The authors are well-known for their own published research in the area.

Knapp, M. L. (1978). *Nonverbal communication in human interaction* (2nd ed.). New York: Holt, Rinehart & Winston.

This revised, second edition of the first undergraduate textbook in the field is lively and easy to read. Research from the social sciences is summarized and applied. Knapp's numerous examples guide the reader through some relatively complex research findings.

Richmond, V. P., McCroskey, J. C., & Payne, S. K. (1991). *Nonverbal behavior in interpersonal relations* (2nd ed.). Englewood Cliffs, NJ: Prentice-Hall.

This text presents an overview of the field. Each chapter is short and highly readable, making it especially appropriate for the undergraduate student. Notable extras in this book (as compared to others on nonverbal communication) are chapters on teacher-student relationships and intercultural communication.

CHAPTER 16

DEVELOPING YOUR OWN RHETORICAL STYLE

Learning Objectives

After studying the chapter, the student should be able to:

- Define and explain the concept of rhetorical style.

- Discuss why it is important to choose a rhetorical style that fits.

- Discuss why a speaker's personal strengths as a communicator should be the basis for selecting a rhetorical style.

- Understand the cautions associated with developing a rhetorical style.

- Identify and develop her or his personal style of communicating with the audience.

- Identify and define four personal communication styles particularly suited for public speaking.

- Identify observable characteristics of each of those four personal communication styles.

- Understand the cautions associated with the humorous style of speaking.

- Understand that there is great variability in how women and men communicate.

- Differentiate between feminine and masculine styles of communicating.

Extended Chapter Outline

This chapter focuses on developing a personal rhetorical style.

I. Discovering Your Own Rhetorical Style
    Rhetorical style is the overall quality of how a speaker communicates using verbal and nonverbal messages.
    A. Choose a Style That Fits You
        A speaker should not try to adopt a style that doesn't fit who he or she is. Inexperienced speakers may have to try several different styles to see which one (or which combination of styles) fits.
    B. Build on Your Own Strengths as a Communicator
        The speaker's personal strengths as a communicator should be the basis for selecting a rhetorical style.

C. Don't Stress Style over Substance

Too much emphasis on style, or how the speaker communicates, without a simultaneous concern for content can misrepresent, mislead, or even undermine the purpose of public speaking.

II. Personal Communication Styles Well Suited to Public Speaking

A. Dramatic Style

Dramatic speakers build tension when they tell a story. They often use colorful words or metaphors, exaggerate for emphasis, and take pleasure joking and playing with the audience. These performers often use magnified gestures and body movements to illustrate their points; they hold eye contact with individuals in the audience a little longer than is comfortable; and they vary their voice over a considerable range to hold attention and create certain effects. Overstatement and understatement are two other strategies used by dramatic speakers. Exaggerating a story to make it seem more than it is or delivering lines with dry wit are examples of these techniques.

B. Animated Style

Energy, enthusiasm, and excitement are the central characteristics of the animated style. Animated speakers exaggerate their nonverbal behaviors by gesturing broadly, smiling frequently, pacing purposefully, nodding knowingly, and raising or lowering eyebrows. Animated speakers show every emotion they feel.

C. Open Style

Speakers characterized by the open style often invite audience involvement and participation by coming across as affable, sincere, trusting, and self-revealing. Generally they take a conversational approach to public speaking. They rely on their personal histories, experiences, and feelings, and are unafraid to show how they feel. Open speakers invite others to display their feelings and attitudes by signaling a receptiveness to others' points of view and through self-disclosure. Most often, such disclosures are positive, but at times the disclosure could reveal negative or personal information that puts the speaker at risk. Overall, speakers who appear sensitive, warm, sympathetic, and understanding are likely to receive audience acceptance and trust. On the other hand, those speakers who come across as remote and aloof are likely to find themselves with an audience that responds in kind.

D. Humorous Style

A humorous style relies primarily on humor to engage audience attention and to build positive affect. Anybody can be funny if they have the opportunity to prepare their humor ahead of time. Humor should be planned and practiced before it is used in a presentation. Speakers can use other people's humorous stories or jokes or recall some of their own personal experiences or ordeals that can be turned into humorous narratives or anecdotes. Audiences like speakers who use humor more than speakers who do not. Humorous speakers are perceived as friendly and audiences generally feel closer to them. Some caution should be used with this rhetorical style:

1. A humor threshold exists for every joke, story, and anecdote.
2. Speakers can try to be *too* funny.
3. The decision to use humor depends on the topic and occasion.

III. Gender-Based Communication Styles

It is important to acknowledge the great variability among women and men and how they communicate. Gender-based communication styles are often attributed to biological sex simply because most adult females today are socialized to be feminine and most males to be masculine, but feminine and masculine styles are not sex-linked. They are merely based on learned sex-role behaviors. Individuals that escape sex-role stereotyping transcend the boundaries of style and flexibly interact as either masculine or feminine communicators.

  A. Feminine Communication Style

    The feminine style of communicating emphasizes interpersonal connection. Feminine communicators seek human connection more than they do status, power, or winning. Such communicators are likely to try to relate to audience members as individuals; they come across as inclusive and immediate. Feminine communicators are also more likely to acknowledge and emphasize areas of agreement between themselves and the audience.

  B. Masculine Communication Style

    The masculine style of communicating is characterized by assertions of status and power by demonstrating strength and independence. No communication event is better suited to the masculine style of communication than public speaking. In their respective roles as speaker and audience, the speaker commands attention, controls the situation, and demands credibility and authority. The audience complies with the speaker's demands. Instead of trying to connect with the audience, masculine communicators are more likely to demonstrate distance and authority by claiming expertise in the subject matter. Rather than relying on personal accounts to demonstrate an idea or support an argument, masculine speakers prefer objective facts, data, and expert testimony.

Classroom Exercises and Activities

1. Have students list both men and women from the media that represent the masculine and the feminine communication styles. Which style of communication commands more audience respect? Which invites relational closeness or friendship? Which style do students prefer their teachers use? Why?

2. Videotape students' speeches for your class. (You could ask your students to bring in their own personal video to record all their own speeches given throughout the semester. In this way, students will have a record to show their improvement as the course progresses.) After privately viewing the playback of one of their own individual videos, each student should provide a written critique of his or her communication style by responding to the following questions and issues:

  a. Label your own communication style in one word or phrase, and explain why you chose that word or phrase.

  b. Based on what you have learned in this course, what do you believe are three of your strengths as public speaker?

  c. What are two of your weaknesses as a public speaker?

  d. How might you improve your weaknesses or capitalize on your strengths as a public speaker? Be specific and behavioral in your answer.

  e. How much of your *true* personality emerged in your presentation? Did you sound sincere, personable, and *real?* Why or why not?

3. Have students generate a list of particularly effective speakers that they know. Ask them to label each speaker's predominant style of communicating (i.e., dramatic, animated, open, humorous, masculine, or feminine). Which style do students like most and least? Why?

4. Have students examine the videotaped speeches that accompany this text. Ask them to identify the predominant communication style of each speaker: David Brashear, Therese Rincon, and Tamara Synigal. Which speaker did they like the best and which the least? Why?

5. Have students identify which style (dramatic, animated, open, humorous, masculine, or feminine) is least like them personally. Have students, in groups of five to seven, attempt to role-play that particular style. Discuss why it is difficult to assume a style that is unlike one's personality.

Recommended Readings

Tannen, D. (1990). *You just don't understand: Women and men in conversation.* New York: William Morrow.

A linguistics professor, Tannen discusses the different ways women and men communicate in her efforts to better understand how the sexes often seem to talk past one another. This very readable bestseller relies on a lot of entertaining examples and anecdotes to demonstrate how women and men can walk away from the same conversation with very different interpretations of what was said or meant.

Norton, R. (1983). *Communicator style: Theory, applications, and measures.* Beverly Hills, CA: Sage.

This upper-division or graduate-level text examines a variety of the communication styles described in this chapter. Of particular interest to students are the self-report questionnaires that Norton uses to assess each style and the rather detailed descriptions of each.

Frank, F., & Anshen, F. (1983). *Language and the sexes.* Albany: State University of New York Press.

This highly readable book looks at how men and women use language differently. This book also makes a political statement: Our society uses language to favor one sex over the other. The authors successfully translate research findings into understandable, interesting, and often humorous reading.

CHAPTER 17

USING VISUAL AIDS

Learning Objectives

After studying the chapter, the student should be able to:

- Define the parameters of the term "visual aids."

- Describe the important role visual aids play in public speaking.

- List and discuss the questions to ask in deciding whether to include a particular visual aid in a speech.

- Understand that the speaker, the nature of the content, and the situation all influence the selection of the most appropriate type of visual aid to use.

- Differentiate among the standard types of visual aids commonly used in public presentations.

- Understand the design composition of a word or text chart.

- Understand the design composition of the four most common types of graphic charts.

- Explain the use of physical representations such as objects, models, and people as visual aids in a public speech.

- Explain the use of visual representations such as photos, maps, and drawings as visual aids in a public speech.

- List and explain all the ways that visual aids can be projected and displayed during a speech.

- Identify the advantages and disadvantages of each method for projecting and displaying visual aids.

- Explain how audio techniques (cassette tapes, compact discs, and records) can be effectively incorporated into a presentation if the objective of the speech invites audio support.

- Identify and apply the nine different guidelines for using visual aids effectively.

Extended Chapter Outline

This chapter focuses on the use of visual aids in public speaking.

I. Visual Aids in Public Speaking
   A. What Are Visual Aids?
      A visual aid is any supplemental visible device that a public speaker employs to help clarify for the audience what is being communicated in a speech.
   B. Deciding Whether to Use Visual Aids

1. Will including visual aids clarify something important for my audience?
   A visual aid clarifies by providing valuable additional information. For example, a speaker might provide photographs of the salient features of a new car. The photographs help the audience understand the features of that car. Actually seeing pictures of the car during the speech clarifies for the audience what the speaker really means.
2. Will including visual aids make my speech more interesting for my audience?
   A visual aid can heighten the interest of an audience by emphasizing an important point in a visually striking manner.
3. Will including visual aids increase my audience's retention of my speech?
   A visual aid can increase audience retention by highlighting what is important to remember in a speech. Visual aids are especially effective when the speaker wants the audience to remember a step-by-step process.
4. Will including visual aids save me valuable time?
   For speech topics requiring a great deal of explanation, the right visual aid can serve as a visual description of one or more parts of the presentation (word picture) and help a speaker explain a topic or idea without having to go into an elaborate discussion and use up valuable time.
5. Will including visual aids help me better organize my speech or will they detract from it?
   The right visual aid can emphasize the organization of a speech by delineating logically the points being covered. An audience can more easily follow a linearly or configurally organized presentation that is laid out visually.

II. Types Of Visual Aids
Public speakers employ many different types of visual aids. The particular speaker, the nature of the content to be presented, and the public speaking situation all influence the selection of the most appropriate type to use. Charts, the most common type, display information in either a tabular or a diagrammatic format.

A. Graphs
Charts that include information in the form of either a graph or some type of picture are referred to as graphic charts. Graphic charts are typically constructed to visualize either statistics or large numbers of similar facts in graphs, diagrams, or tables. The information on these types of charts can be structured to be either two- or three-dimensional in design.

1. Bar graphs
   Bar charts graphically portray quantities or values of different things with a sequence of bars or columns corresponding in height or length to the amount of each item being counted. They are used to depict differences in sets of figures during the same or a shorter time span.
2. Fever graphs
   Fever charts (also called "line graphs"), illustrate graphically how the patterns of things change over time.
3. Pie graphs
   Pie charts (also called "circle graphs" and "divided circle") offer a method of graphically showing the division of the parts of a whole. Pie charts are normally constructed to divide up 100 percent of a circle or pie into sections, each of which represents some percentage of the original pie. Pie charts allow for the visual comparison of the parts of the whole of something at a specific time.

B. Tables
Tables provide public speakers with a way of displaying understandable information in some pattern, such as rankings, categories, or groupings, or other graphic arrangements. Tables allow the speaker to present large numbers of similar pieces of information that cannot be handled by the other graphic visual aids that have been

described. Typically, tables place statistics and other information into columns or a diagram.

C. Charts
Several different types of charts are commonly used as visual aids. In general terms, a chart is a pictorial representation of the relationship between parts of a group or the sequence of steps in a process.

D. Word Charts
Word (or text) charts consist of words, phrases, or short sentences (where no graphic or pictorial material is included) that emphasize the important points in a presentation. The content of these charts is set up around points and subpoints of an outline. This outline is divided up point-by-point and placed in a logical order.

E. Physical Representations
1. Objects
Introducing a physical object during a speech can enhance audience understanding and interest. Objects allow the audience to experience the real thing.
2. Models
Models are scaled-down versions of a larger, unmanageable article. They are useful when the original item is not available.
3. People
Involving one or more people as a type of visual aid is a convenient and effective way to enhance a speech. People can be more effective in demonstration-type speeches than a series of graphic charts.

F. Visual Representations
1. Photos
Photographs can be used to illustrate an important aspect of the speech if they are large enough to see, high in quality, pertinent to the point being communicated, and do not detract from the rest of the speech.
2. Maps
Maps are effective when the speaker wants to illustrate geographic information. To be effective, maps also allow the audience to follow along from one location to another, and to provide directions to some destination. Maps must be large, professional in quality, pertinent to the area or region being described, and introduced and removed at appropriate points in the speech.
3. Drawings
Drawings are an inexpensive and effective way to represent an important idea or concept. They must be prepared before the presentation to ensure proper quality.

III. Presenting Your Visual (and Audio) Aids
A. Projection Techniques
One type of projection is the immobile or fixed approach, or still projection, accomplished with transparencies, slides, opaque projection systems, and filmstrips. Another way to project visual aids is with moving projection, such as films and videotapes.
1. Transparencies
Charts, photographs, maps, and drawings can be copied to or drawn on clear sheets of acetate plastic called "transparencies." Once copied on the transparency, the material can be shown to an audience with an overhead projector system.
2. Slides
Slides are small mounted color transparencies for projecting charts, diagrams, tables, and other images on a screen with a slide projector. The disadvantages of using slides are that they require a projector, which can malfunction, and that for them to be seen the room must be darkened, which can distract from the speaker and the presentation.

3. Opaque projection

Opaque projectors cast a still image on some opaque material like paper directly from a sheet onto a screen. The disadvantages of opaque projection are that it requires a darkened room for maximum clarity and tends to be noisy.

4. Filmstrips

Filmstrips are still images displayed by means of a still-frame filmstrip projector. Certain types of visual aids like charts, photographs, and drawings can be transformed onto a filmstrip.

5. Films and videotapes

Films and videotapes can be employed to heighten an audience's response both to a particular topic and to an action in a presentation. Films and videotapes should be carefully edited to directly support the material in the speech.

B. Displaying Techniques

Display visual aids include handouts, demonstration boards, and flip charts.

1. Flip charts

Flip charts involve a speaker employing a large, simple, and highly visible pad of paper to reveal point by point the major issues of a presentation. Word charts, graphs, diagrams, and tables can be presented to an audience using flip charts. Only one point should be placed on each piece of paper. After the point is made, the speaker flips the paper to the next point. The last page in the sequence is designed to summarize all of the points discussed during the presentation.

2. Demonstration boards

Demonstration boards refer to a group of techniques for displaying information in a public presentation that include the chalkboard, porcelain board, feltboard, and magnetic board.

3. Handouts

Visual aids that are distributed to the audience become handouts. Handouts should be used in only two circumstances: If the material cannot be displayed or projected during a presentation in any other way; or if the audience needs the material for study or reference after the speech.

C. Audio Techniques

Cassette tapes, compact discs, and records can be effectively incorporated into a presentation if the objective of the speech invites audio support. Audio techniques are commonly employed in speeches to incorporate music, interviews of famous people, excerpts from speeches, and background support of one type or another for filmstrips, films, and videotapes. Sound quality must be good, and audio equipment should be checked prior to operation.

IV. Guidelines for Effectively Using Visual Aids

A. Use Visual Aids That Serve a Definite Purpose

Use a visual aid only if a point can be better communicated to the audience visually rather than verbally. Visual aids should never be used solely for their artistic or aesthetic merits.

B. Use Visual Aids That Are Appropriate for Your Speech Topic, Your Audience, and the Occasion

What the speaker is talking about, who the speaker is talking to, and the nature of the speaking situation must all be considered when choosing an appropriate visual aid.

C. Don't Overuse Visual Aids

The primary objectives of employing visual aids in a speech are to clarify, add interest, increase audience attention, save time, and help improve speech organization. These objectives can not be achieved if the audience pays more attention to the visual aids than to the speech or speaker.

D. Use Visual Aids That Require Little or No Explanation

In order to contribute positively to a presentation, visual aids must be simple and clear enough to speak for themselves. Visual aids should stand on their own. Audiences should not need an interpreter to understand the material in a visual aid.

E. Use Visual Aids That Catch and Hold Your Audience's Attention
   Visual aids that command attention are distinctive and professional. Visual aids should look like they required a lot of time and work to construct.

F. Use Visual Aids That Are Easy to See
   Visual aids must be large enough for people in the last row of an audience to see easily. This means not only the overall size of the aid but also the size of the words, graphs, diagrams, and numbers need to be large enough to read easily. Visual aids also need to be positioned, projected, or displayed so that every person in an audience can see them without any difficulty.

G. Keep your Visual Aids in Your Possession during Your Presentation
   Do not give out materials before and during your presentation except under unusual circumstances. Audience members will want to touch or hold an interesting object or follow along on a chart. Do not be persuaded by their demands. Losing your visual aid to the hands and eyes of audience members is a sure way to divert their attention from you and your speech.

H. Remove Your Visual Aids from Sight When You Are Through with Them
   Because quality visual aids tend to distract the audience from listening to the speech, they should be presented at the appropriate time and removed from view after their usefulness is over.

I. Rehearse Using Your Visual Aids Before Your Presentation
   All the preparation in the world and even the highest quality professional aids are no substitute for practice. Effectively rehearsing the use of visual aids means practicing the presentation with the equipment and the aids to achieve correct timing.

Classroom Exercises and Activities

1. We recommend that students develop and use a visual aid for their second major informative speech assignment. Part 4 presents an evaluation form that includes relevant criteria for evaluating the use of visual aids in an informative speech (Informative Speech 2).

2. Collect visual aids that have been used previously by students in your department. Show several examples in class. Evaluate each one based on the guidelines for effectively using visual aids presented in Chapter 17 (i.e., does the visual aid serve a definite purpose? is it appropriate for the topic, audience, and occasion? and so on).

3. Show students one of the videotaped speeches that accompanies this text or have them read one of the student speeches in the Appendix. Have students determine whether or not a visual aid would help or hinder that speech. Their decision should be based on the issues identified in Chapter 17. If your students decide that a visual aid would, in fact, enhance the presentation, what type of visual aid would they select?

4. Have students identify what type of visual aid would be best suited for each of the following topics:

   a. Divorce rates in the U.S. over the last 50 years

   b. The number of employees represented in each department of an organization

   c. Levels of management in the university

   d. Number of violent crimes by type of weapon (gun, knife, club, poison, and so on)

   e. Membership in health clubs by region

f. Variation in chocolate consumption over the last 10 years in the U.S.

g. Alcohol consumption by the general public and ministers' annual incomes

h. Three ways to lose weight

5. Send students to the campus media center and have them list the different kinds of visuals they could use in giving a speech. Have them discover how to check out visual materials for use in the classroom. Report back to the class.

Recommended Readings

Detz, J. (1992). *How to write and give a speech* (2nd ed.). New York: St. Martin's.

Not your typical academic textbook, this is a how-to book that can be purchased in a public bookstore or airport gift shop. Most noteworthy are the short but insightful sections on how to prepare the room for a presentation and how to use audiovisual aids. The material on preparing the room is not typically included in speech texts and is worth examining. The use material includes an interesting discussion of preparing an emergency audiovisual kit that is also worth examining.

Holcombe, M. W., & Stein, J. K. (1983). *Presentation for decision-makers: Strategies for structuring and delivering your ideas.* New York: Lifetime Learning.

This is a good supplemental text on creating and using all types of visual aids in public presentations. The authors effectively detail the specifics of preparing professional-looking charts. They thoughtfully (and in some detail) consider important topics like choosing an appropriate size for the text in charts and provide an extended discussion of the rules and guidelines for designing attractive text and graphic visuals.

Holmes, N. (1991). *Designer's guide to creating charts and diagrams.* New York: Watson-Guptill.

This is an invaluable source on designing charts, graphs, and tables that includes an interesting and readable history of the use of charts and diagrams. The four primary types of charts—fever, bar, pie, and tables—are discussed so that they can be easily constructed for public presentations. There is an unusually good chapter on the uses and misuses of charts. This text includes numerous colorful examples of the four types of charts.

Satterthwaite, L. (1976). *Graphics: Skills, media, and materials* (3rd ed.). Dubuque, IA: Kendall/Hunt.

This introductory text includes an extensive overview of virtually all the formal types of visual aids. The author explains the specifics of audiovisual construction—mounting, illustrating, lettering, duplication, display, use of color, and so on. Chapters are also devoted to techniques for projection and display.

CHAPTER 18

PUBLIC SPEECHES FOR SPECIAL OCCASIONS

Learning Objectives

After studying the chapter, the student should be able to:

- Define and explain a speech of introduction.

- List and discuss the issues important to the preparation of an effective speech of introduction.

- Explain why, with rare exceptions, public speeches for special occasions should be brief.

- Define and explain the different kinds of special occasion speeches described in this chapter.

- List and explain the criteria to use when preparing and evaluating each type of specialized speech.

- Distinguish, in terms of design and delivery, the oral performance of literature and entertaining speeches from other special occasion speeches.

- List and explain the seven rules to help the speaker handle even the most difficult question-and-answer sessions.

- Effectively handle audience questions—even those that can make a speaker defensive.

- Explain the unique experiences that participants have when speaking in small groups.

- List and explain the advantages and disadvantages of small group discussions.

- Differentiate among public discussions, symposia, group or public forums, and panel discussions.

Extended Chapter Outline

This chapter focuses on the presentation of public speeches for special occasions.

I. Ceremonial Speeches
   A. Introductions
      In a speech of introduction, the host provides the audience with sufficient reasons for actively listening to a particular speaker and topic. Introduction speeches should be brief. The following are some important considerations when preparing a speech of introduction:
      1. Get to know some personal firsthand information about the speaker.

2. Use the speaker's name several times during the introduction to ensure that the audience knows the speaker's name and knows how to pronounce it.
3. Establish the speaker's credibility by describing her or his qualifications to talk about the speech topic.
4. Sell the audience on the speaker by explaining why the audience should listen to the speaker.
5. Initiate a good relationship between the speaker and the audience by telling the audience why the speaker is liked.
6. Set the tone for the speaker by letting the audience know what type of speech will be presented.
7. Express sincere pleasure for the privilege of being able to introduce the speaker.
8. Announce the title of the speech.
9. Avoid using trite or overused expressions that detract from the introduction (i.e., "This speaker needs no introduction," "without further ado," and so on).
10. Capture the audience's attention.

B. Welcomes

Welcoming speeches provide a formal, public greeting to a visiting person or group, making them feel comfortable and appreciated in the new and unfamiliar environment. Welcoming speeches extend warm greetings and promote feelings of friendship. They are intended to help visitors feel comfortable by providing them with information about the occasion, about those in attendance, and about the new environment. Welcoming speeches should be brief.

C. Nominations

A formal or public nomination consists of a brief persuasive speech in which an individual's name is publicly forwarded into candidacy. The primary goal of a nominating speech is to lay out the qualities that make the candidate the most credible or suitable person for the award or honor. The nominator should describe the qualities required for all recipients of the award, office, or honor; list the candidate's own personal or professional qualifications that meet those criteria; and designate the nominee by name.

D. Award Speeches

1. Presenting an award

Award speeches are given to present awards recognizing notable accomplishments of an individual or a group for a particular achievement. When presenting an award, the speaker should focus on both the organization bestowing the recognition and the award itself. The qualifications of the recipient and similarities with other honorees should be mentioned. Award speeches should be brief.

2. Accepting an award

In a speech of acceptance, the recipient graciously acknowledges the award and communicates appreciation for having his or her accomplishments recognized. An acceptance speech should convey a sincere expression of appreciation for being honored and recognized. Within reason, all those that made the accomplishment possible should be thanked. The speaker should never apologize for receiving an award or use the opportunity to advance or draw attention to some other social or political cause. Acceptance speeches should be brief.

E. Tributes

A tribute is a speech publicly acknowledging major or long-term accomplishments of an individual or a group. Tribute speeches are intended to honor far-reaching and highly symbolic accomplishments. They are often presented on special holidays that are designated as public opportunities to celebrate notable accomplishments of individuals and groups or those associated with pivotal events.

1. Eulogies

   A eulogy is a speech praising or honoring an individual's accomplishments given for someone who has recently died. Eulogies must be genuine and sincere, and decorum and self-control must be maintained. A good eulogy makes the individual being honored memorable by including either a personal story or a vivid anecdote about the person. Eulogies should be brief.

2. Toasts

   A toast is a very short speech of tribute. It is appropriate at any formal or informal occasion where someone's achievement or accomplishment is being celebrated. A toast should be brief and set a tone of good cheer; generally toasts are given in a conversational, yet eloquent speaking style. They should focus on some positive attribute of the person receiving the mini-tribute.

F. Commencement Speeches

   Commencement speeches are presentations delivered at graduation exercises in which a speaker praises and congratulates individuals who have formally completed a prescribed set of educational requirements. Commencement speeches are highly complimentary. Begin preparation of a commencement speech by describing, recognizing, and celebrating the significance of the special occasion. Then praise those graduating and acknowledge those in the audience for their support. Finally, challenge those who are graduating to look ahead and to consider the important roles they can play in society.

G. Dedications

   Dedication speeches bestow or commit some new commodity to an ideal or value, like improved community relations, good service, or community development. Dedications are appropriate at special occasions that celebrate the beginning of something new, as when new buildings or facilities are opened. Dedications should be short, acknowledge the contributions of those involved, and describe how what is being dedicated symbolizes a certain idea or value.

H. Farewells

   One type of farewell speech is a short presentation in which a person who is leaving ceremonializes his or her goodbye. In the second type, a presenter communicates a brief ceremonial goodbye and gives a sendoff to a departing person.

   1. A farewell speech given by the person departing should express sentiments of pleasure, gratitude, and fondness for the long-term association with friends and colleagues and the opportunity to serve the group; she or he should also thank those celebrating the departure. A farewell speech allows the audience to experience the presentation vividly through metaphors, similes, and intense, animated language.

   2. A farewell speech given for someone departing should acknowledge his or her contributions by giving a sincere and enthusiastic thank-you for all they accomplished in the past. Praise should address specific achievements and accomplishments. The formal farewell speech should conclude on a positive note by wishing the individual good luck.

II. Other Types of Specialized Public Presentations

   A. Oral Performances of Literature

      The oral performance of literature helps to set the stage and the agenda for celebrating a special occasion. While the nature of the material being presented dictates the organization and design of the oral performance, certain rules govern this activity in all situations:

      1. The length of the presentation depends on the length of the material; however, brevity and succinctness are important.

      2. Introductions to such presentations should include the title of the selection, the author's name, and the overall theme of the written work.

3. The speaker should set the appropriate mood by including any background material relevant to the characters and setting.
4. The body of the presentation should be consistent with the theme and appropriate to the particular audience.
5. The oral performance should be delivered in a highly expressive way.
6. The performance should be rehearsed until it is committed to memory.
7. The manuscript should be treated as a prop, used to remind the audience that the presentation is a literary performance.
8. The audience should be left with a "gee-whiz" experience.

B. Entertaining Speeches

Speeches to entertain (also called after-dinner speeches) attempt to get an audience to enjoy an interesting presentation in a relaxing, lighthearted, and enjoyable atmosphere, often through the creative use of humor. This type of speech is more like persuasive and informative speeches in the completeness of organization and design than most special occasion speeches. Any topic can be made into an entertaining speech. Humor should be based on a thorough audience analysis.

1. Effective entertaining speeches contain witty illustrations, humorous anecdotes, and recollections of unique and amusing experiences.
2. Entertaining speeches rely on how something is said and require an animated, dramatic delivery style.
3. Speakers planning an entertaining speech should thoroughly rehearse and plan to pause for applause and laughter.

C. Question-and-answer Sessions

The following are seven time-proven rules that can help the speaker strategically handle even the most difficult question-and-answer sessions.

1. Solicit questions from all parts or sections of the audience. This ensures that every member of the audience has equal status and something important to inquire about.
2. Listen carefully to each question before responding. Speakers often fail to really listen to what an audience member is asking or what may be the hidden agenda driving the question.
3. Repeat aloud all positive questions and when possible, rephrase, reword, or paraphrase all negative or loaded questions. Repeating the question gives the speaker the opportunity to make sure the question is understood before responding. Rewording a negative or loaded question in a more neutral or positive way minimizes the chance of a possible adverse reaction to the answer from the audience.
4. When responding to negative or loaded questions, give eye contact to the audience in general as opposed to looking directly at the questioner. Questioners that ask loaded questions are trying to make the speaker look bad. By avoiding direct eye contact with the questioner, the speaker can diffuse other person-specific efforts to make the speaker look bad to the audience.
5. If the answer to a question is not known, it is better and safer to say so. Audiences interpret such honesty as a strength rather than a weakness.
6. Give answers, not lengthy sermons or lectures. Keep answers brief and to the point.
7. Be pleasant and polite at all times. Maintaining composure under tense or stressful circumstances helps audience members perceive the speaker as credible and believable.

D. Speaking in Groups

Small groups are composed of three to eight people who engage in face-to-face interaction around some common purpose or objective. Participants in small group discussions normally experience a sense of belonging that alters the way they communicate.

1. Disadvantages of small group discussions
   The most obvious disadvantage is the pressure to conform to the norms of the group. Additionally, one member may dominate the group interaction, allowing participants to rely on the attitudes of the dominating member. Finally, groups often waste time while making decisions. These disadvantages are obstacles to reaching the most effective solution to a problem in the shortest amount of time.
2. Advantages of small group discussions
   Small groups are very effective in problem-solving situations because they bring more knowledge and information about the topic than would be expected of any one individual. Groups tend to be more creative than individuals. Satisfaction tends to be greater with group participation than for individuals working on the same task alone. The following are four well-used formats that govern the type of public speaking that can occur in group discussions:
   a. Public discussions
      Public discussions involve a predesignated group of individuals interacting and exchanging ideas about a particular topic while seated in front of an audience.
   b. Symposium
      A symposium is a public presentation in which a series of short, preplanned speeches about a topic are delivered to an audience.
   c. Group forum or forum presentation
      In a group forum or forum presentation, audience members advance questions to the entire group; individual group members then answer the questions.
   d. Panel discussion
      A panel discussion involves an organized and moderated group presentation to an audience.

Classroom Exercises and Activities

1. Throughout the course, it's a good idea to have students practice a number of special occasion or ceremonial speeches. Evaluation forms for a number of these presentations are available in Part 4 of this manual, including: a speech of introduction, a speech giving an award, a speech accepting an award, giving a toast, a eulogy, a pet-peeve speech, an impromptu persuasive speech, and an oral performance of literature. With the exception of the literature performance, all of these speech assignments are 1- or 2-minute minor presentations.

2. Videotape an awards ceremony from television: Oscars, Emmys, Tonys, Golden Globe, MTV, the Grammys, People's Choice, VH1, American Music, Black Entertainment Award, or other similar award. Have students analyze three specialized speech types: speeches of introduction, speeches giving an award, and speeches accepting an award. To what extent did the entertainers follow the guidelines from the text? Which presentations were most or least effective? Why?

3. Have students observe a specialized presentation in their own community or on campus. Ask them to write a detailed critique analyzing that presentation relying on criteria from the text.

4. Give your students the following list of negatively worded or loaded questions. Have them assume that someone from the audience asked them one or more of those questions. Ask them to generate responses that they might use to successfully reframe the question in an effort to minimize an adverse audience reaction.

   a. Do you believe abortion is the murdering of helpless, unborn children?

b. How many times have you verbally or physically abused members of your family?

c. Why should the media continue to show pornography all day long?

d. Why don't you support gays and lesbians in the military?

e. Why should illegal aliens receive medical benefits?

f. Do you think illegals belong in this country?

g. Do you support non-English versions of social service exams?

h. Why should we continue to support minority quotas?

i. As a supporter of the war, would you send your own child to fight?

j. As a self-acclaimed religious person, you should support pro-life groups—right?

k. As a supporter of the death penalty, would you be willing to take responsibility for murdering an innocent person?

Recommended Readings

Lee, C. I., & Gura, T. (1987). *Oral interpretation* (7th ed.). Boston: Houghton Mifflin.

This popular text offers a complete introduction to the study and practice of the oral performance of literature. Each chapter is written to blend theory with practice. Pertinent topics discussed include the use of voice, language, and imagery and handling difficult material and other issues important to presenting literature effectively. The text offers a number of suggestions that are particularly helpful for polishing this type of presentation.

Ratliff, G. (1981). *Beginning readers theatre: A primer for classroom performance*. Annandale, VA: Speech Communication Association.

Similar to the available oral performance texts, this book covers a number of topics relevant to refining the content of specialized presentations in general. It makes a number of substantive recommendations for using language and the voice that apply to all types of performance.

Vital Speeches of the Day. Mount Pleasant, SC: City News Publishing.

This bimonthly periodical publishes the original texts of all types of contemporary speeches, including special-occasion speeches. Each text is unaltered and authentic. The speeches published here provide the opportunity for students to examine firsthand how speakers of all types polish and refine their presentations.

Cathcart, R. S., & Samovar, L. A. (eds.) (1988). *Small group communication: A reader* (5th ed.) Dubuque, IA: William C. Brown.

This is an excellent compilation of basic articles on communication in groups. Now in its fifth edition, this reader has remained popular for over two decades. Essays include discussion of group environments, decision making, group presentations, leadership, and evaluation. Each article is well written and easy to read. This text is a valuable supplement to any course in group communication.

Goodall, Jr., H. L. (1990). *Small group communication in organizations* (2nd ed.). Dubuque, IA: Wm. C. Brown.

This introductory text provides a straightforward overview of small groups in American organizations. In simple language the author discusses the basics of small group processes, as well as participation and communication in small groups plus leadership in the small group. Numerous examples help the student work through the material. This book is very suitable for the introductory student interested in making presentations in groups.

Detz, J. (1991). *Can you say a few words?* New York: St. Martin's.

This excellent supplement to introductory classes in public speaking will help students interested in understanding the basics of speaking on special occasions. The author discusses the elements of more than twenty different types of speeches. Each section is written in simple language and serves as an excellent quick reference when preparing for a brief specialized speech. The author also discusses how to use humor when speaking and how to answer questions from the audience.

Gresham, P. E. (1985). *Toasts: Plain, spicy, and wry.* Ocoee, FL: Anna Publishing.

This is literally a book of various kinds of toasts. This author has effectively pulled together a large number of toasts suitable for every imaginable occasion. Beginning with a discussion of the history of toasting, the author presents toasts appropriate for family, professional, international, and a host of other types of gatherings.

PART 4

EVALUATING STUDENT SPEECHES

PHILOSOPHY OF EVALUATION

Evaluating student speeches is perhaps the most difficult part of the teacher's job. Some teachers are too easy with grades, others too hard. Some evaluate speeches based on student effort; others on some objective standard; still others on improvement. Whatever approach you take to evaluating student speeches, you should know what you're doing and why you're doing it, and you should apply that approach consistently across all students.

In case you're not sure what your own position is on grading speeches, we offer you our own position. It's taken many years for us to develop this perspective. In every decision we have made, we provide our reasoning. Take what works for you; revise what doesn't until you're comfortable with your own approach.

1. *Students should be aware of the specific criteria that you will use to grade them before their actual performance.* Students perform better if they know how they will be evaluated. We shouldn't expect our students to guess what's in our mind; they should know up front exactly what they're expected to do (and not do). Give students their speech evaluation form on the day the speech is assigned; go over each criterion; and explain that they can expect an A if all criteria are met. Ask them to bring their evaluation form with them on the date of their speech so you can use it.

2. *Speech criteria should be specific and behavioral.* The more specific and concrete the criteria are, the more likely students will be able to practice and perfect those skills. At the same time, precise and observable standards also help you increase your own effectiveness at rating student presentations. Taking the subjectivity out of grading helps make your evaluations more reliable and accurate. It also helps you defend an evaluation when a student questions one.

3. *Speech criteria should become increasingly more difficult for each new speech assignment.* Learning a speech skill, like learning many other complex activities, is incremental. You may want to begin evaluating speeches early in the course by listing a minimal number of different behavioral skills that your students must master, such as "gives eye contact," "gestures purposefully," or "has an identifiable introduction, body, and conclusion." As your students become more proficient and more relaxed in front of the class, you will want to add increasingly more difficult criteria. With each new speech evaluation form, prior criteria are subsumed. (The speech evaluation forms that we designed for this manual are based on the incremental method, with minor speech evaluation forms relying primarily on delivery skills and major forms relying more on content and organization. See below.)

4. *Students need a lot of positive reinforcement.* Find something to like about every speech and speaker and comment on it. Sometimes it's more important for speakers to know what they're doing right than what they're doing wrong. Avoid making generic comments, like "Good job!" Instead, make your comments specific and personal to that speech, like "Your use of transitions between major headings worked really well." For every negative (or constructive) comment you make, think of three positive remarks. Positive reinforcement works better on humans (and animals) than punishment.

5. *Negative feedback should be given in a constructive manner that shows students where improvement is needed and how to go about doing it.* Constructive feedback implies what the student did wrong without having to explicitly spell it out. Constructive feedback helps the student save face and avoid embarrassment. As with positive feedback, constructive feedback should be specific and behavioral. Tell the student exactly what to do next time: "You need to spend more time developing the need or problem with the status quo. For this speech, you spent about 20 seconds; for your next speech, plan on 60 seconds or more."

6. *Regardless how poor the performance, focus on only two or three specific areas that need improvement.* Some students have a longer way to go than others before meeting all the criteria for a good speech. There may be much you can offer them in the way of constructive criticism. But it is important not to overwhelm them with comments. Expect them to work on only two or three things; if there are more, they will feel helpless and discouraged.

7. *Give specific feedback about speech performance privately to students in writing.* Try not to embarrass a particular student by using her or him as an example to the entire class. Interestingly enough, this advice holds for positive comments as well. Many students, especially those high in communication apprehension, are likely to feel embarrassed with such attention, even if it's intended to be positive.

8. *Return speech grades the same day.* Inexperienced public speaking teachers have difficulty accomplishing this task—listening to the speaker, timing the speech, making comments on the evaluation form, totaling the points, and assigning the grade—all in a matter of minutes! With practice, you can do this, and there are plenty of reasons why you will want to do so. First, you are more likely to evaluate the speech accurately when the performance is fresh in your mind. Second, students want their grades right away. Research shows that immediate feedback results in greater behavioral change; students will see right away what you saw and try to correct it. Third, potential grade disputes can be handled more easily (see number 9).

   In order to facilitate a quick turnaround, have a student in class record the time (and provide time signals to the speaker). Use an evaluation form that provides a checklist or point system (see our evaluation forms below) that can be easily used and scored. Keep written comments brief and to a minimum. Remember: Too much feedback is likely to overwhelm. Don't use more than 1 or 2 minutes between presentations to make comments. While you are totaling points, have the next assigned speaker for that day getting ready.

9. *Tell students that disagreements about their speech grades must be settled that day.* Our syllabus (see Part 1) requires that all speech grade disputes be settled on the actual day of performance. With the speech fresh in your mind, you are better able to objectively defend or change your evaluation of a particular performance.

10. *Once the speaker starts, let him or her finish.* This advice probably goes without saying, but we've actually heard of teachers interrupting their student speakers, commenting on what they did wrong, and requiring them to begin again. Such interruptions only

cause the speaker more anxiety. The only time a speaker should stop and start from the beginning is when the student wants to.

11. *Students late for class should wait outside until after the speaker is finished.* Unanticipated interruptions can rattle even the best speaker by increasing performance anxiety. Our syllabus (see Part 1) addresses this point. Everyone should come to class on time and be ready for the first student performance. Students who cannot make it to class (for whatever reason) should not interrupt the speaker, but wait to enter the classroom after the speaker is finished with his or her performance.

12. *Student peer evaluations should not be used unless students are taught how to evaluate.* Research on peer evaluations of student speakers suggests that, without guidance and structure, they vary wildly (Bohn & Bohn, 1985). Unreliable peer evaluations are likely to undermine your own assessments of the speaker's performance as most students overestimate the speaker's abilities. Some teachers, however, find that peer input gives the speaker additional feedback and reinforcement. If you choose to provide peer evaluations to student speakers, *train* the audience how to evaluate. Give them specific, behavioral criteria that they should focus on. Keep the criteria to a minimum. Practice having them evaluate a videotaped speaker. Help them achieve a reliable, valid assessment of speech performances.

13. *Audience members should follow each presentation with applause.* In most professional settings, audience members provide the speaker with enthusiastic applause when he or she concludes. In this simulated context, it's a good idea to have the audience do the same. This helps achieve a supportive climate for each speaker.

14. *Provide general feedback at the end of the class session, not after each individual speaker.* Once again, you'll find some teachers who like to make comments immediately following each and every speaker. We like to hold comments until the last 5 minutes of each class session for two reasons: It saves time, and it takes the pressure off any individual student. When you do make comments, make sure that your feedback is primarily positive and that any negative feedback is worded constructively. For instance, "With this round of speeches, the attention-getters are really getting to be quite creative. What were some strategies our speakers used today?" And "I want to see you all work on providing a clear preview in your introduction. Use signposts to help us follow along."

SPEECH EVALUATION FORMS: Instructor Evaluation

In keeping with the philosophy of evaluation that we've outlined above, we prefer to use very specific, behavioral assessments. What follows are a series of evaluation forms. The first set can be used to assess major or 5- to 8-minute speeches:

1. Informative Speech 1
2. Informative Speech 2 (includes criteria for using a visual aid)
3. Persuasive Speech (based on Monroe's Motivated Sequence)
4. Oral Performance of Literature

The second set of evaluation forms is designed to assess minor or 1- or 2-minute specialized presentations:

1. Speech of Introduction
2. Giving an Award
3. Accepting an Award

4. Giving a Toast

5. Eulogy

6. A Pet-Peeve Speech (emphasizes delivery skills)

7. Impromptu Persuasive Speech

Our evaluation forms are based on a rating scale and a point system. In this way, each behavioral criterion can be rated from 1 to 5; points can be easily totaled; and final grades can be assigned quickly. Specific comments can be written on the form (or on   back), although we encourage you to keep your comments brief.

You may choose to use any of these forms or any revision of them. Experiment with different formats and change the criteria to meet the particular needs of your students as they begin to develop the requisite speaking skills. Remember to give your students a copy of your evaluation form on the day you assign the speech; in this way, students will know exactly what to expect and be in a better position to do what you want.

INFORMATIVE SPEECH 1
30 points   .

NAME: _____

INTRODUCTION (15)	AGREE				DISAGREE
Captures audience attention	5	4	3	2	1
Alerts audience to central idea or purpose	5	4	3	2	1
Provides clear preview or road map	5	4	3	2	1

BODY (20)					
Uses transitions and signposts	5	4	3	2	1
Points supported with facts	5	4	3	2	1
Points supported with personal accounts or experiences	5	4	3	2	1
Organizational logic or pattern makes sense	5	4	3	2	1

CONCLUSION (10)					
Reviews the main points	5	4	3	2	1
Provides a memorable conclusion	5	4	3	2	1

DELIVERY (15)	YES		NOT YET	
Competent: knowledgeable in subject	3	2	1	0
Trustworthy: open and sincere	3	2	1	0
Composed: confident and in control	3	2	1	0
Sociable: smiles and gives eye contact	3	2	1	0
Extroverted: purposeful gestures and movements	3	2	1	0

OUTLINE REQUIRED: Typed and in outline form

TIME LIMIT (5 min.)   _____

Penalty Points   _____

Speeches presented without a typed outline will result in a penalty of 4 points subtracted from your final speech grade. Similarly, presentations that do not conform to the time constraint of 5 minutes (plus or minus 30 seconds) will result in a penalty of as many as 4 additional points.

Total Points (60 possible) _____

divide by 2   _____

minus penalty points   _____

YOUR SCORE   _____

INFORMATIVE SPEECH 2
30 points

NAME: _____

INTRODUCTION (10)	AGREE			DISAGREE	
Captures audience attention	5	4	3	2	1
Provides clear preview or road map	5	4	3	2	1

BODY (15)					
Uses transitions and signposts	5	4	3	2	1
Points supported with facts and personal experiences	5	4	3	2	1
Organizational logic or pattern makes sense	5	4	3	2	1

CONCLUSION (10)					
Reviews the main points	5	4	3	2	1
Provides a memorable conclusion	5	4	3	2	1

DELIVERY (10)	YES		NOT YET
Appears confident and in control	2	1	0
Smiles and gives eye contact	2	1	0
Uses purposeful gestures and movements	2	1	0
Vocally expressive	2	1	0
Delivery is truly extemporaneous	2	1	0

VISUAL AIDS (10)			
Communicates idea visually	2	1	0
Simple and uncomplicated	2	1	0
Professional quality	2	1	0
Large enough to see	2	1	0
Displayed when appropriate (and then removed)	2	1	0

OUTLINE (5)			
Typed and in correct outline form	2	1	0
At least two references	2	1	0
Written in correct APA style	2	1	0

TIME LIMIT (5 min.) _____

Penalty Points (±30 sec.) _____

Total Points (60 possible) _____

divide by 2 _____

minus penalty points _____

YOUR SCORE _____

PERSUASIVE SPEECH
30 points

NAME: _____

GAINS AUDIENCE ATTENTION (5)	AGREE			DISAGREE	
Creative attention-getter	5	4	3	2	1

IDENTIFIES UNFULFILLED NEEDS (15)

States need or problem explicitly	5	4	3	2	1
Documents the extent of the problem	5	4	3	2	1
Creates tension in the audience (the need to know)	5	4	3	2	1

IMPLIES SATISFACTION BY OFFERING A SOLUTION (20)

Waits to provide explicit solution now	5	4	3	2	1
Explains how solution works	5	4	3	2	1
Relates solution back to needs (tells how solution solves the problem)	5	4	3	2	1
Overcomes objections	5	4	3	2	1

VISUALIZES WHAT SATISFACTION WILL MEAN (5)

Visualization is concrete, vivid, and personal	5	4	3	2	1

DEFINES SPECIFIC ACTIONS (5)

Steps are specific and concrete	5	4	3	2	1

DELIVERY

Verbal communication: (5)	YES	NOT YET
Verbally immediate	1	0
Uses metaphors or similes	1	0
Uses intense, animated language	1	0
Employs inclusive language	1	0
Maintains rhythm (repeats and rephrases)	1	0
Nonverbal communication: (5)		
Clothing establishes credibility	1	0
Varies speech rate and volume	1	0
Purposeful body movements	1	0
Uses exaggerated illustrators	1	0
Nonverbally immediate	1	0

OUTLINE

Penalty Points   _____

Outlines must be typed, in correct format, and with at least two references documented in APA
style. Speeches presented without meeting these requirements will result in a loss of up to 4 points.

TIME LIMIT (5 min.)   _____

Penalty Points   _____

Presentations that do not conform to the time constraint of 5 minutes (±30 seconds) will
result in a penalty of up to 4 points.

Total Points (60 possible)   _____

divide by 2   _____

minus penalty points   _____

YOUR SCORE   _____

ORAL PERFORMANCE OF LITERATURE
30 points

NAME: _____

INTRODUCTION (NARRATION) (15)	AGREE			DISAGREE	
Gives author and title of the selection	5	4	3	2	1
States theme	5	4	3	2	1
Sets the mood (gives background information re: character and setting)	5	4	3	2	1

BODY (THE LITERATURE) (10)					
Literature fits the theme	5	4	3	2	1
Selection is appropriate for the audience	5	4	3	2	1

DELIVERY (30)					
Facially expressive	5	4	3	2	1
Reflects appropriate emotion	5	4	3	2	1
Vocally expressive	5	4	3	2	1
Bodily expressive	5	4	3	2	1
Obviously well-rehearsed	5	4	3	2	1
Manuscript is handled effectively	5	4	3	2	1

CONCLUSION (5)					
Provides memorable conclusion	5	4	3	2	1

TIME LIMIT (8 min.) _____

Penalty Points _____

Presentations that do not conform to the time constraint of 8 minutes (±60 seconds) will result in a penalty of up to 4 points.

Total Points (60 possible) _____

divide by 2 _____

minus penalty points _____

YOUR SCORE _____

SPEECH OF INTRODUCTION
5 points

NAME: _____

SPEECH CONTENT	AGREE				DISAGREE
Pronounces name correctly	5	4	3	2	1
Gives credibility to the introduced speaker	5	4	3	2	1
Spurs interest in the speaker's topic	5	4	3	2	1
Expresses personal pleasure in being able to introduce the speaker	5	4	3	2	1
Sounds well-rehearsed and has clever transition to the speaker	5	4	3	2	1

SPEECH DELIVERY*					
Gave eye contact to entire audience	5	4	3	2	1
Smiled at audience	5	4	3	2	1
Avoided nervous mannerisms	5	4	3	2	1
Conversational style	5	4	3	2	1
Vocally expressive	5	4	3	2	1

*Points are assigned for the content criteria only, not for delivery. The total points for content divided by 5 equals your score. The speech delivery information is used for feedback purposes only. However, a perfect score of 25 will result in 1 extra point for this speech.

TIME LIMIT (60 seconds) _____

Total Points _____

GIVING AN AWARD
5 points

NAME: _____

SPEECH CONTENT	AGREE		DISAGREE		
Names the organization giving the award	5	4	3	2	1
Describes values represented by the award	5	4	3	2	1
Describes the selection process	5	4	3	2	1
Mentions the qualifications of the recipient	5	4	3	2	1
Shows how this recipient is similar to other award-winners	5	4	3	2	1

SPEECH DELIVERY*					
Gave eye contact to entire audience	5	4	3	2	1
Smiled at audience	5	4	3	2	1
Avoided nervous mannerisms	5	4	3	2	1
Conversational style	5	4	3	2	1
Vocally expressive	5	4	3	2	1

*Points are assigned for the content criteria only, not for delivery. The total points for content, divided by 5 equal your score. The speech delivery information is used for feedback purposes only. However, a perfect score of 25 will result in 1 extra point for this speech.

TIME LIMIT (60 seconds) _____
Total Points _____

ACCEPTING AN AWARD
5 points

NAME: _____

SPEECH CONTENT	AGREE			DISAGREE	
Accepted the award graciously	5	4	3	2	1
Gave credit to others	5	4	3	2	1
Humble, but no false modesty	5	4	3	2	1
Thanked those who bestowed the award	5	4	3	2	1
Complimented the competition	5	4	3	2	1

SPEECH DELIVERY*					
Gave eye contact to entire audience	5	4	3	2	1
Smiled at audience	5	4	3	2	1
Avoided nervous mannerisms	5	4	3	2	1
Conversational style	5	4	3	2	1
Vocally expressive	5	4	3	2	1

*Points are assigned for the content criteria only, not for delivery. The total points for content divided by 5 equals your score. The speech delivery information is used for feedback purposes only. However, a perfect score of 25 will result in 1 extra point for this speech.

TIME LIMIT (60 seconds) _____

Total Points _____

GIVING A TOAST
5 points

NAME: _____

SPEECH CONTENT	AGREE			DISAGREE	
Focused on some positive attribute or characteristic of the person	5	4	3	2	1
Relied on a personal story or anecdote that demonstrated the point	5	4	3	2	1
Created a vivid, memorable image of the person being honored	5	4	3	2	1
Came across as sincere and genuine	5	4	3	2	1
Set the tone	5	4	3	2	1
SPEECH DELIVERY*					
Gave eye contact to entire audience	5	4	3	2	1
Smiled at audience	5	4	3	2	1
Avoided nervous mannerisms	5	4	3	2	1
Conversational style	5	4	3	2	1
Vocally expressive	5	4	3	2	1

*Points are assigned for the content criteria only, not for delivery. The total points for content divided by 5 equals your score. The speech delivery information is used for feedback purposes only. However, a perfect score of 25 will result in 1 extra point for this speech.

TIME LIMIT (60 seconds) _____

Total Points _____

EULOGY
5 points

NAME: _____

SPEECH CONTENT	AGREE			DISAGREE	
Points out what was significant and good about the person	5	4	3	2	1
Praises the individual's deeds	5	4	3	2	1
Expresses sorrow or deep regret	5	4	3	2	1
Attempts to comfort the group	5	4	3	2	1
Makes the person memorable by relating a personal story or anecdote	5	4	3	2	1

SPEECH DELIVERY*

Sets a respectful tone	5	4	3	2	1
Gave eye contact to entire audience	5	4	3	2	1
Vocally expressive	5	4	3	2	1
Maintains appropriate decorum or self-control	5	4	3	2	1
Responsive to audience	5	4	3	2	1

*Points are assigned for the content criteria only, not for delivery. The total points for content divided by 5 equals your score. The speech delivery information is used for feedback purposes only. However, a perfect score of 25 will result in 1 extra point for this speech.

TIME LIMIT (60 seconds) _____

Total Points _____

PET-PEEVE SPEECH
5 points

NAME: _____

SPEECH CONTENT	AGREE			DISAGREE	
Identifiable introduction, body, conclusion	5	4	3	2	1
Sounds well-rehearsed	5	4	3	2	1
Establishes an initial positive impression	5	4	3	2	1
Uses nonverbal immediacy behaviors:					
Physical closeness	5	4	3	2	1
Eye contact	5	4	3	2	1
Smiling	5	4	3	2	1
Head nodding	5	4	3	2	1
Illustrators:					
Purposeful gestures	5	4	3	2	1
Forward body lean	5	4	3	2	1
Uses verbal immediacy behaviors	5	4	3	2	1

TIME LIMIT (60 seconds)   _____

Total Points   _____

SCORE (total divided by 10)   _____

Persuasive Impromptu

Instructions: This persuasive impromptu speech exercise was created many years ago by Madeline MacDonald, a teaching assistant at California State University, Sacramento. This clever format will help your students understand the basics of performing a persuasive, as opposed to an informative, speech. For this impromptu speech, students should be given a notecard with two comparable objects, events, or issues. With minimal preparation time, the student must select one of the two (X) and argue convincingly to the audience why it is somehow better than the other (Y). Here are some sample comparisons you could use:

Pizza vs. hamburgers
Jogging vs. swimming
Giving a gift vs. receiving a gift
Blue vs. red
Spring vs. fall
Winter vs. summer
Living in the East vs. the West
Living in the North vs. the South
New York City vs. Los Angeles
Dogs vs. cats
Being short vs. being tall
Blondes vs. brunettes
Hairy vs. hairless
Long hair vs. short hair
Cars vs. trucks
Live plants vs. artificial ones
Apples vs. oranges
Foreign cars vs. American cars
Your birthday vs. Christmas (or another holiday)
Sweaters vs. sweatshirts
Going to a movie vs. renting a video

Arriving early vs. arriving late
Wine vs. beer
Majoring in speech vs. business
Frozen yogurt vs. ice cream
Coke vs. Pepsi
Loafers vs. tennis shoes
Staying up late vs. getting up early
Rap vs. rock 'n roll
Daytime vs. nighttime
Kids vs. adults
Rural vs. city life
Large families vs. small families
Dirty vs. clean
Hot vs. cold
Fitness vs. thinness
Women vs. men
Pens vs. pencils
Renting vs. buying a home
Home state vs. another state
Traveling by airplane vs. train
Walking vs. jogging
Watching TV vs. reading a book

PERSUASIVE IMPROMPTU
5 points

NAME: _____

SPEECH CONTENT	AGREE				DISAGREE
Provides an appropriate attention-getter	5	4	3	2	1
Establishes a need for *both* X and Y	5	4	3	2	1
Explicit statement of claim that X is better than Y	5	4	3	2	1
Cites reasons why X is better than Y	5	4	3	2	1
Reiterates claim that X is better than Y	5	4	3	2	1

SPEECH DELIVERY*					
Uses verbal and nonverbal immediacy	5	4	3	2	1
Good voice projection	5	4	3	2	1
Projects enthusiasm	5	4	3	2	1
Content flows easily	5	4	3	2	1
Ending is not abrupt	5	4	3	2	1

*Points are assigned for the content criteria only, not for delivery. The total points for content divided by 5 equals your score. The speech delivery information is used for feedback purposes only. However, a perfect score of 25 will result in 1 extra point for this speech.

TIME LIMIT (50–70 seconds) _____

Total Points _____

SPEECH EVALUATION FORM: Student/Peer Evaluation

Earlier we cautioned you against using student evaluations of presentations. Our concern stems from the research that demonstrates that student ratings of speeches are highly unreliable and thus invalid. With training and supervision, however, you can teach your students how to reliably evaluate a student speech. Begin by providing them with an evaluation form that includes specific behavioral criteria. To ensure that students focus on key behaviors, keep the list of criteria short. (Do not have them use the same evaluation form that you use; yours will be far too comprehensive for them to accurately employ.) Go over the criteria with them in class— teach them what to look for; show them instances and non-instances of what you mean. Have them watch a videotaped presentation of a speech and rate the speech and speaker; and then discuss their responses in class. With repeated practice sessions, students can be taught to reliably observe and record those behaviors you want them to. What follows is a sample peer evaluation form that you might want to use or revise.

PEER EVALUATION FORM

SPEECH CONTENT:	AGREE			DISAGREE	
Introduction (10)					
Introduction gains my attention	5	4	3	2	1
Preview is specific	5	4	3	2	1
Body (10)					
Main points are signposted	5	4	3	2	1
Supporting evidence is used for each main point	5	4	3	2	1
Conclusion (10)					
Summarizes main points	5	4	3	2	1
Concludes with a memorable statement	5	4	3	2	1
SPEECH DELIVERY (20)					
Smiles at audience	5	4	3	2	1
Gives sustained eye contact	5	4	3	2	1
No nervous mannerisms	5	4	3	2	1
Loud enough for everyone to hear	5	4	3	2	1

Total Points _____

PART 5

SAMPLE STUDENT SPEECHES FOR ANALYSIS AND DISCUSSION

Three speeches delivered by three different student speakers are presented in the video that accompanies this text. The first two speeches are both informative speeches on the same topic and content. However, the first speaker, Euroamerican David Brashear, presents his informative speech using a linear organizational pattern, whereas Latina Therese Rincon presents her informative speech using a configural organizational pattern (see Chapter 12). Our third student speaker, African American Tamara Synigal, presents a persuasive speech that follows Monroe's Motivated Sequence. In this section of the manual, we present the actual speech outlines that each of these speakers employed to deliver their respective speeches, followed by an analysis that you can use to inform your students as they watch the videotape.

Following that material, we offer an analysis of the three student speeches presented in the Appendix of the text. These speeches were prepared and delivered in introductory public speaking classes at California State University, Long Beach. The first speech is informative; the second and third are persuasive. You might ask students to outline one or more of these speeches to see how well they follow a recognizable organizational pattern. You might also ask them to critique the written text—what was good about the speech; what would they have done differently if they were to deliver that speech?

SPEECHES ON VIDEOTAPE: OUTLINES AND ANALYSES

1. Informative Speech: Linear Organization

Title: "The Coffee House Craze"

Speaker: David Brashear

Specific Purpose: To inform my audience about the growing coffee house phenomenon.

Thesis Statement: In order to understand the role of coffee houses in society today, we need to look at the history of coffee houses, the people who frequent them, and the jargon that's unique to them.

OUTLINE

Introduction

Attention-Getter:

The *Utne Reader* calls it the "most popular unregulated drug in America." In fact, 52 percent of us make this indulgence part of our daily ritual. This ritual is not only taking place just in our homes, but in chic public settings. Grandmas, students, couples, singles, and artistic Bohemians all answer to the call of "Order! One double espresso caffe mocha!" That's right: The indulgence I'm talking about is coffee. Now more than ever we are flocking to coffee houses, where the drinks are as complex as they sound and the atmosphere is fashionable.

Preview:

Even though all of us may not be avid coffee drinkers, or perhaps there are those among us who don't like coffee at all, you will still find that coffee houses have something to offer you. Today I'd like to (1) share with you the history of coffee houses, (2) talk about the people who frequent them, and (3) provide you with some coffee house terminology.

[Transition: Let's begin by tracing the history of coffee houses.]

Body

I. The History of Coffee Houses
   A. The origin of coffee houses dates back to 17th-century Europe. The first known coffee houses were in Italy and London.
      1. Earlier coffee houses functioned as a meeting place to exchange local and world news.
      2. The postal service and the public used coffee houses to collect and deliver letters.
      3. The popularity of these early coffee houses dwindled in the late 19th century as more nightclubs, hotels, and restaurants began to flourish.
   B. The coffee shops of the 1950s sprouted a resurgence. With bright neon road signs and bold architecture, they provided a place for family dinners, after-school hangouts, and business meetings. The coffee houses of the 50s are not to be confused with the coffee houses of today.
      1. Coffee shops of the 50s offered full service.

2. Coffee houses today have a limited menu, if any.
C. Starbuck's, the Seattle-based chain, is credited with the reintroduction of coffee houses. Coffee bars of the 90s are quaint structures that aim to sell not only coffee and atmosphere, but merchandise.
   1. Many provide couches and other comfortable seating. The coffee houses of today promote lingering which, in turn, yields more consumption of coffee.
   2. While some coffee house chains sell only beverages, others sell books, cards, coffee mugs, t-shirts, and other coffee lovers' paraphernalia.
   3. Some coffee houses boost their business by providing live entertainment. Guitarists, singers, jazz ensembles, and poetry readings are part of the weekly calendar.
   4. The 1994 October issue of *Consumer Reports* states that less than 5 years ago, there were fewer than 200 coffee bars in the U.S. But today, there are over 5000! And by the year 2000, that number is expected to double!

[Transition: With these rising numbers, let's take a look at the people who are making this business boom.]

II. The People
   A. Like the coffee houses of the 17th century and the coffee shops of the 50s, today's coffeebars attract all kinds of people.
   B. In Ken Ohlson's 1993 article, "Bean Scene," baby boomers, high school and college students, and even teens are the most likely patrons.
      1. Teens and high school students like coffee houses because it provides them with a savvy atmosphere. But they really like them because there is no drinking age requirement.
      2. With hard alcohol on the decline, baby boomers and young adults have turned to coffee drinks. And, instead of going to nightclubs to meet that *special someone*, many are finding that coffee houses provide a much more sobering atmosphere to interview a prospective date.

[Transition: Coffee house regulars have no problem ordering their drinks, but for many of us, ordering a specialty coffee drink can be a point of great trepidation.]

III. Coffee House Lingo
   A. With drinks called "latte" or "espresso," it is enough to make us order just a plain cup of coffee and feel like a real failure. The 1994 October edition of *Consumer Reports* kindly defined the three most popular variations:
      1. First, there's espresso: "It's a dark roast, finely packed coffee that is brewed in a special coffee maker—in other words, it's strong! Espresso is also the starting point for a lot of specialty coffee drinks."
      2. Cappuccino: A combination of 2 ounces of espresso blended with steamed milk and topped with frothed milk or whipped cream.
      3. Caffe latte: A single shot of espresso to which steamed milk is added. Lattes can be flavored with Italian syrups, like almond or hazelnut.
   B. Now for those of you who still are not tantalized with such exotic sounding drinks, coffee houses provide alternative beverages, such as hot chocolate, fruit juices, and herbal teas.

Conclusion

Summary:

Today we talked briefly about the history of coffee houses, their patrons, and brushed up on our coffee house lingo.

Memorable statement:

Even though you may never order a double tall, skinny, blended latte on the rocks with a dash of hazelnut, the coffee house offers something for everyone. And, on that note . . . it's time for a coffee break!

REFERENCES

A business built on beans. (1994, October). *Consumer Reports*, p. 642.

Hess, A. (1986). *Googie: Fifties coffee shop architecture.* Vancouver, BC: Raincoast Books.

Lillywhite, B. (1963). *London coffee houses.* London: George Allen and Unwin Ltd.

Middleman-Thomas, I. (1994, March). Cafe ole. *Hispanic*, p. 38.

Ohlson, K. (1993, December). Bean scene. *Entrepreneur*, pp. 90–93.

Schapiro, M. (1994, November/December). Muddy waters. *Utne Reader*, pp. 58–65.

Slaves to the grind. (1993, October). *Rolling Stone*, pp. 51–52.

The coffee achievement. (1994, December 19–26). *New York*, p. 71.

ANALYSIS

David's introduction is dramatic, not only in his words and phrases, but in his nonverbal communication as well. He is both direct and assertive. Notice his change in vocalics, his subtle use of pauses, and his gestures for emphasis. David speaks like a Euroamerican: His preview is explicit; he uses exact statistical facts in his introduction and throughout the remainder of his speech; and he directs the audience to his first main point with a transition statement. David is forthright and direct; he avoids using qualifiers. By using the words "we" and "us," he makes an effort to be inclusive and connect with his audience.

The body of David's speech is organized in a topical linear pattern with three main points (I, II, III), subpoints, and sub-subpoints. Notice how in his first main point, the history of coffee houses, he organizes his subpoints in a chronological order. David again cites facts and numbers and gives credit to a variety of sources. In his efforts to remain inclusive, David concludes the body of his presentation by making one final attempt to recognize those in his audience who do not drink coffee (III-B).

His conclusion includes both an explicit summary and a clever memorable statement. The audience wanted to hear more.

Besides preparing an excellent speech on coffee houses, complete with a good list of references, David Brashear's delivery overwhelmed his audience. His presentation was a show-stopper! He came across as credible, believable, confident, and composed. David has a clearly definable personal style of communicating: dramatic. He tells a good story and seems to enjoy performing.

2. Informative Speech: Configural Organization

Title: "The Coffee House Craze"

Speaker: Therese Rincon

Specific Purpose: To inform my audience about the growing coffee house phenomenon.

Thesis Statement: We can look at the coffee house phenomenon from a variety of perspectives: its resurgence, the fact that coffee houses are nothing new, the coffee house crowd, and coffee house terminology.

OUTLINE

Introduction

Attention-Getter:

The *Utne Reader* calls it the "most popular unregulated drug in America." Supposedly half of all Americans make this indulgence part of their daily ritual. This ritual is taking place not only in our homes, but in public as well. Students, teens, aspiring artists, and even members of our own family are answering to the call of "Order! One double espresso caffe mocha!"

Preview:

It seems as though we are flocking to coffee houses, where the drinks are complex and the atmosphere is fashionable.

Body

I. Current Resurgence of Coffee Houses
   A. Starbuck's, the Seattle-based chain, is credited with starting this new wave of coffee bars. The coffee houses as we know them today are often designed to provide a comfortable atmosphere.
      1. Because of such a warm atmosphere, customers are in no hurry to leave.
      2. Many coffee bars offer books and other coffee items for sale. Customers often take the time to leisurely browse.
      3. Some coffee houses provide entertainment. Customers are treated to instrumental music, vocalists, or poetry readings on a weekly basis.
   B. The fondness for coffee houses appears to be growing. The 1994 October issue of *Consumer Reports* stated that less than five years ago, there were no more than 200 coffee bars in the U.S. Today that number has exceeded into the thousands. And by the year 2000, the numbers are expected to double.

II. Coffee Houses Are Nothing New
   A. Coffee houses can be linked to the coffee shops of the 1950s as well as the coffee housesof the 17th century. These original coffee houses surfaced in Europe.
   B. The early coffee houses provided meeting places for people to share local and world news. The postal office as well as the public used coffee houses to collect and deliver letters.

C. With their bold architecture and bright neon road signs, coffee shops of the 50s attracted all kinds of people. The coffee houses of the 90s, like those in the 50s, share a commonality for unique design and style. However, coffee shops of the 50s offered full-service dining.

III. The Coffee House Crowd
   A. Coffee houses today, much like their predecessors, cater to a diverse crowd.
   B. Ken Ohlson's 1993 article, "Bean Scene," states that the most prosperous coffee houses are near high schools and college campuses as well as corporate business areas.
   C. Coffee houses appeal to a lot of people.
   1. Today heavy drinking is becoming passé.
   2. Coffee bars are also popular because they have no drinking age requirement.
   3. Singles have found that the atmosphere provides a somewhat safer environment to meet new people.

IV. Coffee House Terminology
   A. There are so many drinks served in coffee houses that it sometimes is difficult to really know what you are ordering. Many of us end up ordering just a plain cup of coffee.
      1. Take, for example, espresso: It is a dark roast finely packed coffee that is brewed in a special coffee machine. It can be served plain or with a topping of frothed milk.
      2. Cappuccino combines 2 ounces of espresso with steamed milk. This drink is also topped with frothed milk or whipped cream.
      3. Caffe latte is a single shot of espresso blended with steamed milk. Lattes are often flavored with Italian syrups like almond or hazelnut.
   B. Coffee houses not only sell coffee, but hot chocolate, herbal teas, as well as an assortment of fruit juices.

Conclusion

Summary:

Even though you may never order a double tall, skinny blended latte on the rocks with a dash of hazelnut, the coffee house has plenty to offer. Coffee houses of the past like the present provide a comfortable atmosphere to chat with friends, find entertainment, and enjoy a good cup of coffee.

Memorable Statement:

And on that note . . . I think it's time for a coffee break.

REFERENCES

(same list as David's)

ANALYSIS

Therese's introduction differs sharply from David's. Characteristically Latina, Therese's approach is much more indirect and implicit. Aware of the same statistical facts as David, Therese substitutes exact numbers with a more qualitative bent ("half" rather than 52%), not only in the introduction, but throughout her entire text ("thousands" rather than 5,000). A careful examination of her word choices reveals a degree of tentativeness as well ("it seems as though," "supposedly"). Her preview is so implicit and inexact that the audience is required to infer what she intends to say. Therese maintains her indirectness with her implied summary as well.

Therese's informative speech outline follows a configural, multiple-perspectives format. Coffee houses are viewed from a variety of different perspectives. To fully understand coffee houses today, she tells us about coffee houses in the past, the kinds of people who frequent coffee houses, and the terminology associated with ordering a cup of coffee. Only with multiple perspectives can the audience appreciate what coffee houses mean.

Unlike David, Therese does not follow a systematic chronological order in her historical overview of coffee houses. Her first main point begins with coffee houses today. It's not until her second main point that she discusses the historical antecedents of coffee shops. Back and forth, she discusses the coffee houses of earlier years with those of today. A concern with the past blended with the present characterizes much of the speech's subtext.

Throughout her speech, Therese implies where David was explicit and direct. For instance, Therese allows the audience to infer that coffee houses cater to teens, college students, and business executives by specifying where prosperous shops are located (III-B). She implies that ordering complex drinks like lattes and espressos can be anxiety producing without directly saying so (IV-A). She merely hints at the needs and concerns of non-coffee drinkers (IV-B). Contrast her indirectness with David's rather explicit detail.

A quick overview of Therese's delivery style suggests a high-context speaker. Her paralanguage, gestures, smiling, eye contact, forward body lean, and other nonverbal behaviors all illustrate a reliance on what she says nonverbally. Therese comes across as warm, open, and sincere. Her credibility ratings would probably be highest on the sociability and extroversion factors. Her personal rhetorical style is overwhelmingly open and immediate; her energy level and enthusiasm also reflect an animated style.

3. Persuasive Speech: Monroe's Motivated Sequence

Title: "Powering Ourselves"

Speaker: Tamara Synigal

Specific Purpose: To persuade my audience to start walking for a healthy heart.

Thesis Statement: Because people today enjoy far too much a sedentary lifestyle at the expense of their health, they should get out and start walking.

I. Attention
  A. Let's be frank: We are all living the good life. The 20th century has provided us with cars, dishwashers, TVs, stereos with remote controls, automatic door openers—you name it—we've just about *powered* everything. Flip a switch, clap your hands, press a button: Who could ask for more?
  B. Yet today's luxuries have turned us into passive, lethargic—we have all heard the term— *couch potatoes!*
II. Need
  A. The 1994 October issue of *Health* magazine stated that adults watch between 15 and 18 hours of TV a week—meaning we spend approximately "40% of our leisure time in front of the TV."
    1. The ironic twist, *Health* magazine also reports, is that we really don't like many of the shows we watch.
    2. With all our leisure time spent doing nothing but just watching TV, you would think we would feel relaxed and at ease. Not so.
  B. Kathleen McAuliffe's article "Out of the Blues" reports that our sedentary lifestyle is bad for our mental and emotional state of mind.
    1. McAuliffe states that "12.6% of Americans suffer from anxiety and another 9.5% suffer from serious depression."
    2. In the early 18th and 19th centuries, work and life were much more difficult and demanding. Yet studies today indicate that people are experiencing higher bouts of depression.
  C. The lax lifestyle of the 20th century is not only affecting mental health, it's killing us off in alarming numbers.
    1. The 1991 *Encyclopedia of Visual and Natural Healing* states that "more Americans die from heart attacks than any other cause."
    2. The American Heart Association reports that "approximately 500,000 men and women die from heart attacks each year."
  D. Our eating habits combined with our lack of exercise is purported to be the "second leading non-genetic contributor to death in the U.S."
    1. We tend to eat foods that are high in fat, which produce high levels of cholesterol in our blood, which in turn leads to plaque in our arteries.
    2. Think about it: Those 20 hours a week spent watching TV are filled with buttered popcorn, heaping bowls of ice cream, or the chocolate bars bought to help out a fund-raiser.
    3. Modifying our diet can certainly help us decrease our risk for heart disease. But studies have also indicated that people who don't exercise are at an even greater risk for heart disease.

III. Satisfaction
   A. Fortunately, there is one form of exercise we can all do. It is so simple and yet so effective.
      1. Not only that, it is relaxing and, at the same time, energizing. It can help relieve tension and stress from everyday life.
      2. It requires no health club membership; it's cheap; it's portable; it requires very little training; and you're not left gasping for breath.
   B. It's called walking. Walking is one of the most natural behaviors we engage in; yet often overlook its power. Simple walking for 20 minutes at a moderate pace 3–4 times a week is good for our heart, our health, and our state of mind.
   C. When practiced regularly, it can greatly reduce our risk for heart disease.
      1. 1994 article titled "Feet First Prevention" reported that walking can curtail our risk for heart disease.
      2. Blood fats called "triglycerides" are linked to premature hardening of the arteries. Yet the article reported that walking enhances "an enzyme in the blood and muscle that snatches triglycerides from our bloodstream."

IV. Visualization
   A. We can continue to take shortcuts in life: look for the closest parking slot at the mall; drive to the mini-mart around the corner; or spend hours on the phone talking to friends who probably live close by. Sure, these shortcuts save time but, in reality, we are short-circuiting our heart and our health.
   B. Or we can choose to lessen our risk for heart disease, anxiety, and depression by making an effort to walk. Walking will enable you to stumble onto natural little wonders that otherwise go unnoticed. John P. Wiley comments on the benefits of walking by stating,
      "Being on your own two feet is restful. No one is climbing on your back, leaning on a horn designed to blast an opening a mile ahead . . . and if something [or someone] catches your eye, you can stop without being rear ended."

V. Action
   A. I want you to start walking. That's right. Simply walk. It's that easy.
   B. Let's start walking to the store, to the park, to the market. Let's start walking for leisure and for our life.
   C. Instead of watching that half-hour sitcom show that we don't even enjoy, let's do something our hearts will: Walk!

REFERENCES

Bowen-Shea, S. (1994, May/June). Walking shorts. *Walking*, 8–10.

Carey, B. (1994, October). Turn off the T.V. *Health*, 82–84.

Feinstein, A. (1991). *The encyclopedia of visual and natural healing*. Pittsburgh, PA: Rodale.

McAuliffe, K. (1994, March/April). Out of the blues. *Walking*, 42–47.

Ullman, S. A. (1994, January). Feet first prevention. *Prevention*, 9–10.

Wiley, Jr., J. P. (1989, July). Phenomena, comments and notes. *Smithsonian*, 22–24.

ANALYSIS

Because Tamara's speech is persuasive, she organized her presentation using Monroe's Motivated Sequence. All five steps are included. The attention step motivates the audience to listen; they can't help but wonder where she's going with her idea that everything is "powered" these days. In fact, the audience may initially assume that Tamara is going to persuade them to give up television viewing. Not so; there's no potential for psychological reactance with this introduction.

Tamara spends a lot of time establishing the need, or the problem with the status quo. She relies on quotes, credible sources, and statistics to demonstrate that a sedentary lifestyle is bad for our mental and physical health—it could even cause us to die young! Clearly, the need is well substantiated. Notice that throughout the need step, Tamara never once mentions the solution.

She continues to build suspense in the initial stage of the satisfaction step—what kind of exercise requires no health club, is cheap and portable, and demands little training or effort? In this way, she attempts to inoculate her audience by raising potential objections and refuting them. Her solution is explicit and clear: walking. She tells the audience how long to walk and how many times a week they should walk. She then illustrates how and why walking can curtail heart disease, but she falls short of explaining how her solution impacts emotional health (one of the needs expressed earlier).

Her visualization includes both negative and positive consequences to the absence or presence of her solution. Her action step reveals exactly what the audience needs to do right now, right away. Notice how she relates her conclusion to her opening remarks.

In terms of delivery, Tamara is a powerful speaker: Like David, Tamara's communication style is both dramatic and humorous. Notice how in the attention step, she claps her hands, flips an imaginary switch, and presses an imaginary button in the air. Tamara magnifies her nonverbal gestures, facial expressions, and body movement, all adding emphasis and drama to her verbal message. Several times you can hear the audience laugh aloud; you get the sense that both Tamara and the audience are enjoying themselves.

SPEECHES IN TEXT'S APPENDIX: ANALYSES

1. Informative Speech

Title: "The Healing Nature of Mime

Speaker: Patrick McLoy

Patrick began his presentation with a rather unusual attention-getter: a mime performance. There wasn't a sound in the room as he began his performance—everybody listened! Importantly, everybody seemed to understand the message he was trying to convey nonverbally. But just in case they didn't, he told them verbally the essence of what he intended to convey ("Don't let life pass you by, for in the end, you will die"). Patrick's preview was explicit: two main points will be covered. While dramatic, his speech introduction was too long for the time allotted for this presentation; as a result, he had to rush through the body of his speech.

Patrick used transitions to move into his first main point and again to enter his second. He had several expert sources for his points, but he also relied on himself for evidence, offering personal testimony on the benefits of mime.

His closing remarks included a rather brief summary that he extended with an emotional, moving, and relevant story. He even concluded with a short, but memorable statement ("Now you're living. Now you're living").

Patrick has mastered the dramatic style of communicating: His introduction (although too long) and conclusion were both memorable and motivating. Patrick needs to work more on the substance or body of his next speech: Spell out the main points and subpoints; then provide sufficient evidence and examples to illustrate each and every one.

2. Persuasive Speech

Title: "Television Can Be Murder"

Speaker: Mehdi Safaie

Not unlike Patrick's, Mehdi's attention-getter was dramatic and memorable. Mehdi's story of a small boy murdered by two other children stimulated in his audience both horror and interest in his topic. The fact that the murderers had seen a video depicting a similar crime prior to their own killing stirred further outrage. Important to persuasion, however, is thwarting potential psychological reactance. Mehdi may have stimulated some resistance by hinting at a causal relationship between the video and the murder so early in his attention step.

The need step clearly establishes a problem with the status quo. Relying on a number of experts in the field, Mehdi demonstrates that "there is absolutely no doubt" that television violence is somehow related to viewer aggression. To Mehdi's credit, he recognizes that some in the audience may not believe in a causal link; he is quick to address those concerns with a rather simple, yet believable analogy (smoking and cancer).

At the satisfaction step, Mehdi offers a clear and simple solution prefaced with a signpost: "The key word is responsibility." Notice how often he repeats "responsibility" throughout the remainder of his presentation—adding emphasis and increasing the chances of retention. Mehdi's solution doesn't ask the audience for too much change—he doesn't recommend television censorship or industry regulation. Instead, he wants parents and media to assume responsibility.

Visualization is accomplished with the facts (2% reduction). But the recommended action is vague and imprecise: Exactly how does Mehdi want the audience to monitor their television viewing? Unless he provides his audience with a way to implement the solution (take responsibility), the audience is left guessing and wondering just what they should do.

3. Persuasive Speech

Title: "Take a Stand for Human Rights"

Speaker: Charles Park

Charles's attention step is also dramatic. He tells his story effectively by using concrete images; intense, animated language; the active voice; and power phrases. The audience is immediately pulled into the action. And he builds suspense: What did I do to deserve this kind of terrible treatment? When he finally reveals the crime, the audience can't help but be repelled: That's just not fair! Charles brings the story closer to home by revealing the victim's name, Alicia Partnoy, whom he claims, represents "tens of thousands of people around the world."

The magnitude of the problem becomes even clearer during the need step. Charles couples his emotional story with hard facts and statistics. Notice Charles's attempts to be inclusive and to make the problem personal: "These things are happening to people like you and me."

The solution is finally offered—at first indirectly (he identifies the mission and accomplishments associated with Amnesty International) and later directly (he urges people to join this organization and write letters). To show how the solution works, Charles completes the story of Alicia Partnoy—Amnesty International worked for her.

Visualization is brief: "If it wasn't for individuals writing to the oppressors of human rights, people such as Alicia might not be allowed to tell their story today." But the action step is direct and extensive. That is, Charles offers a variety of ways for the audience to help. Each suggestion is concrete and feasible.

Charles leaves the audience thinking with a quote that calls on everyone to do their patriotic and moral duty and take a stand against oppression. He makes it seem as though all "32 of us" can actually do something about this problem.

PART 6

EVALUATION AND FEEDBACK

EVALUATING STUDENTS

All teaching involves evaluation, at the heart of which is making judgments about how to measure achievement. To be sure students have learned, a teacher must observe or test students' performance in some way. Bloom, Hastings, and Madaus (1971) divide measurement of achievement into two categories: formative and summative.

Formative measurement occurs before or during instruction. It has two basic goals: to guide the teacher in planning and to help students identify areas to study. Tests or observations of performance closely related to learning objectives are useful for this purpose (Woolfolk & McCune-Nicolich, 1984). Summative measurement occurs at the end of a sequence of instruction. Its purpose is to let the teacher and students know the level of achievement acquired. The final comprehensive exam and teacher evaluations given at the end of the course are examples of summative feedback.

The difference between formative and summative evaluation is really one of purpose or use. If the goal is to obtain information about achievement in order to plan future lessons, the testing is formative. If the purpose is to measure final student achievement or the teacher's overall performance, the evaluation is summative. Let's now look at some common formats of formative tests: objective and essay exams.

Writing Exam Questions

Objective Testing. Multiple-choice, true-false, matching exercises, short-answer questions, and fill-in items are all objective tests, meaning that items are not open to many interpretations or the questions are not subjective. When objective tests are used, the most difficult part is writing the items. (Essay tests also require careful construction, but the major difficulty with essays generally is grading the completed answer.) Before we turn to essays, let's discuss some guidelines for constructing and grading multiple-choice (not multiple guess) tests. The guidelines we have provided rely heavily on Gronlund (1982) and Woolfolk and McCune-Nicolich (1984). Importantly, we relied on these guidelines in constructing the 1,100+ examination questions in the Test Bank for this text.

1. The *stem* of a multiple-choice item is the part that asks the question or poses the problem. The choices are called *alternatives*. The wrong answers are called *distractors* because of their purpose.

2. The stem should be clear and simple and present only a single problem. Unessential details should be left out.

INCORRECT:

There are several cultural factors that seem to make a difference in how people communicate. The cultural factor that emphasizes family, ingroups, and cooperation is commonly referred to as _____.

CORRECT:

The cultural factor that emphasizes family, ingroups, and cooperation is called _____.

3. The problem in the stem should be stated in positive terms. Negative language is confusing. However, if you must use words such as "not," "no," "false," or "except," underline them or type them in all capitals.

INCORRECT:

Which of the following is not an advantage of speaking from a manuscript?

CORRECT:

Which of the following is NOT an advantage of speaking from a manuscript?

4. As much wording as possible should be included in the stem so that phrases will not have to be repeated in each alternative.

INCORRECT:

A speech about how people can recycle trash to conform with community guidelines would most likely be categorized as:
a. a speech to persuade.
b. a speech to inform.
c. a speech to entertain.

CORRECT:

A speech about how people can recycle trash to conform with community guidelines would most likely be categorized as a speech to:
a. persuade.
b. inform.
c. entertain.

5. Do not expect students to make extremely fine discriminations.

INCORRECT:

Most researchers claim that _____ percent of a message's impact is due to nonverbal factors:
a. 93
b. 95
c. 85

CORRECT:

Most researchers claim that approximately _____ percent of a message's impact is due to nonverbal factors:
a. 90–95
b. 60–65
c. 35–40

6. Each alternative answer should fit the grammatical form of the stem so that no answers are obviously wrong.

INCORRECT:

The statement "the world is round" is an example of a:
a. fact.
b. attitude.
c. belief.

CORRECT:

The statement "the world is round" is an example of a(n):
a. fact.
b. attitude.
c. belief.

7. Categorical words such as "always," "all," "only," or "never" should be avoided unless they can appear consistently in all alternatives. Using these categorical words is an easy way to make the alternative wrong, but most smart test takers know they ought to avoid categorical answers.

INCORRECT: High communication apprehensive students:
a. never receive extra help or prompts from the teacher.
b. are always perceived as more intelligent.
c. are perceived as detached and apathetic toward school.

CORRECT: High communication apprehensive students:
a. receive extra help or prompts from the teacher.
b. are perceived as more intelligent.
c. are perceived as detached and apathetic toward school.

8. The distractors (wrong answers) should be the same length and in the same detail as the correct alternative.

INCORRECT:

Which function of a speech does the phrase "In summary" fulfill?
a. to remind your audience to pay attention, so they can remember what they are supposed to do
b. the conclusion
c. to remind the audience of your main points

CORRECT:

Which function of a speech does the phrase "In summary" fulfill?
a. to end the speech in an upbeat manner
b. to sign off, leaving the audience wanting more
c. to remind the audience of your main points

9. Avoid including two wrong answers (distractors) that have the same meaning. If only one answer can be right and two answers are the same, then they both must be wrong. This narrows down the choices.

10. Avoid using the exact wording of the textbook. Poor students may recognize the answers without knowing what they really mean.

11. Avoid overuse of "all of the above" and "none of the above." Such choices can help students who are simply guessing. In addition, "all of the above" may trick a quick student who sees that the first alternative is correct and does not read on to discover that the others are correct, too.

12. Obvious patterns also aid students who are guessing. The position of the correct answer should be varied, as should its length. The correct answer should sometimes be the longest, sometimes the shortest, and more often neither the longest nor the shortest.

13. In your directions to students, you may want to suggest that they select the "best" answer to each question, as opposed to the "right" answer. This may help to avoid those lengthy discussions about whether the correct answer was really correct or whether several of the other options might be correct as well.

Essay Testing. Essay testing allows students to create answers on their own. Some learning objectives are best measured by this type of evaluation. The most difficult part of essay testing is judging the quality of the answers, but the importance of writing good, clear questions should not be easily dismissed. Let's examine how essay tests should be the written, administered, and graded.

1. Essay tests should be limited to measuring more complex learning outcomes (synthesis, application, and evaluation), which cannot be measured by short objective questions. For example,

   Explain why a persuasive speech needs a different format than an informative speech for maximum effectiveness.

2. An essay question should give students a clear and precise task. It should indicate the elements to be covered in the answer. For example,

   Explain Monroe's Motivated Sequence. Be sure to discuss the five steps in correct order.

3. Give students ample time for answering. If more than one essay is being completed in the same class, you may want to give suggested time requirements for each. For example,

   1. Differentiate between informative and persuasive speaking. (10 minutes)

   2. Explain the theory of psychological reactance and how reactance influences audience response. (15 minutes)

4. Do not include a large number of essay questions. It is better to plan on more frequent testing than to include more than two or three essay questions in a single class period.

5. Combining an essay question with a number of objective items is one way to avoid the problem of limited sampling.

Taking the Subjectivity out of Grading. Prior research has demonstrated that subjectivity in grading essays and papers is widespread among educators. For example, Starch and Elliott (1912) completed a series of studies that found that the same papers given to different teachers to evaluate produced scores ranging from 64 to 98 percent. That is, the grades for the same papers ranged from D to A. Neatness, spelling, punctuation, and communication effectiveness were evaluated differently by each teacher. Follow-up studies found that these results were not confined to one subject area. Rather, the individual standards of the grader and the unreliability of scoring procedures caused the primary problems (Starch & Elliott, 1913a, 1913b, cited in Woolfolk & McCune-Nicolich, 1984).

Furthermore, certain qualities of an essay itself were found to influence grades. For example, in a study of grading practices of 16 law schools, Linn, Klein, and Hart (1972) found that neatly written, verbose, jargon-filled essays with few grammatical and construction errors were given the best grades. Other research indicates that teachers often reward quantity (verbosity) rather than quality in essays (Woolfolk & McCune-Nicolich, 1984, p. 552).

There are several ways to avoid the problems of subjectivity and to ensure fairness and accuracy in grading essays:

1. Construct a model answer first. That is, you should outline the answer you expect your students to provide.

2. Preassign various point values to each part of the answer.

3. You may also want to assign points for the organization and internal consistency of the answer.

4. Once you have assigned points, translate each value into a grade such as 1 to 5 or A, B, C, D, and F.

5. Sort the papers into piles by grade. The papers in each pile should be skimmed to see if they are relatively comparable in quality. What you're searching for here is internal consistency or reliability in your grading.

6. Grade all responses to one question before moving to the next.

7. After you finish reading and scoring the first question, shuffle the papers so that no students end up having all their questions graded first, last, or in the middle (Hill, 1976).

8. Ask students to put their names on the back of their papers, so that grading is anonymous.

How to Assign Grades

There are a variety of ways you can compute and assign grades for your class. We have outlined some of the more common ways teachers determine final course grades. The first, norm-reference grading, is used by most teachers and understood best by most administrators, students, and parents. However, it may not be the most appropriate grading method, particularly if your class is small and your students do not reflect the entire range of abilities evidenced in the normal population. College students, on the whole, represent a skewed distribution of abilities and achievements—most have a history of obtaining Cs or better in school. To impose a normal curve onto students who are already abnormal, that is, high achievers, is inappropriate.

Criterion-reference grading is one of the best approaches, as you will see below. After all, this method requires that students achieve at some standard that you set beforehand. The criteria are spelled out before the student even enters the classroom, so that both you and the student know what it takes to make an A, B, C, D or F.

The point system is an alternative that can be used in conjunction with either norm- or criterion-reference grading systems. It's an easy way for both you and your students to keep track of grades as the semester goes along simply by keeping score. The syllabus supplied in this manual relies on the point system.

Norm-Reference Grading. In norm-reference grading, the major influence on a grade is the student's standing in comparison with others who also took the course. One very popular type of norm-reference grading is grading on a curve or using a normal distribution. If grading were done strictly on the normal curve, there would be an equal number of As and Fs, a larger number of Bs and Ds, and an even larger number of Cs.

Criterion-Reference Grading. In criterion-reference grading, the grade represents a list of accomplishments. If clear objectives have been set for the course, the grade may represent a certain number of objectives that have been met satisfactorily. When a criterion-reference system is used, criteria for each grade are set in advance. It is then up to the student to strive for and reach a level that matches the grade she or he wants to achieve. In this system all students can achieve an A if they master the necessary number of objectives. Conversely, all students could fail to achieve any or all objectives, depending on the inherent difficulty of the tasks involved. Criterion-reference grading has the advantage of relating judgments about a student to the achievement of clearly defined learning objectives.

Point-System Grading. The point system is a popular method for combining grades from many assignments. Each test or assignment is given a certain number of total points, depending on its importance. A test worth 25 percent of the final grade could be worth 25 of 100 total potential points earned in a course (or 50 of 200 points). Points are then awarded on the test or assignment based upon specific criteria. The criterion-reference and point-system methods may be combined, as we do in the sample syllabus. Using a point system has several advantages. First, it is easy to calculate final grades. Second, it is easy for the students to keep track of their own progress. Finally, it helps teachers determine the relative weights or worth of each class activity or assignment.

Guidelines for Assigning Grades

We know that calculating and assigning grades are the least agreeable activities for any teacher. You can have a really good class, generate a lot of enthusiasm, and build positive affect with students—up until the first speech evaluation or exam. At that point, students may become irritable, angry, and even hostile if they feel you have been unfair or unreasonable in your grading practices. To save yourself some of this negative feedback and to ensure that everyone understands your grading policies, we suggest you practice the following tips (modified from Drayer, 1979, pp. 182–187).

1. Explain your grading policies to students the first day or the first week in the course. Remind them of your policies regularly; students may forget or need to be told more than once. Be sure to include your grading policy on your course contract or syllabus.

2. Set reasonable standards.

3. Base your grades on as much objective evidence as possible. *Participation* is subjective and may suffer from teacher bias. For example, attractive, outgoing students receive more attention and better grades than unattractive, quiet students. In some cases, however, the talkative student is perceived as a *problem student*, while the quiet one is thought to be the *perfect student*. Obviously then, the communication behaviors of students in the classroom affect the perceptions made about them, and thus their participation grade. If you really want to grade participation, perhaps you should consider doing in-class activities, with each activity representing a certain number of points in the class.

4. Be sure students understand test and assignment directions. You may want to write out the instructions on a handout or outline them on the board.

5. Ask clear questions focusing on important material that has been taught.

6. Watch for cheating during tests. Do not leave the classroom. Walk around the room; let your students know you are attentive, but not hounding them. Be firm but reasonable when you encounter cheating.

7. Correct, return, and discuss tests as soon as possible. Turnaround time should be no longer than one week. Remember: Students like (and expect) immediate feedback.

8. As a rule, do not change a grade unless you make a clerical or calculation error. Make sure you can defend the grade assigned in the first place.

9. Guard against bias in grading. You may want students to put their names on the back of their papers or use an objective point system when grading essays or papers.

10. Keep students informed of their class standing. Of course, if you use a point system, students can easily keep track of their own records.

11. Give students the benefit of the doubt. All measurement techniques involve error. Unless there is a very good reason not to, give the higher grade in borderline cases.

12. Review your exam questions or assignment. If a large number of students miss the same question or part of an assignment in the same way, revise the question or assignment for the future and consider throwing it out for that assignment. When you admit your errors to students, they are more likely to perceive you as flexible, responsive, and ethical.

EVALUATING TEACHERS

Students aren't the only ones who are evaluated; teachers, too, are graded on their performance in the classroom. Sometimes these grades or evaluations may not seem all that fair. Some students, for instance, may complain that you are not available during office hours, when in fact, you are always there. The point is, you may be right, but if students don't *perceive* that you are available (at their convenience), then they may indicate on your evaluations that you are not. Other responses, however, may be more accurate than you may want to admit. Treat your evaluations and students' written comments as constructive criticism to help you become better at what you do. Try not to get too ego-involved and defensive. Even though negative feedback hurts, you will still want to know what you do wrong and how to become a more effective teacher in the long run.

Remember also, that teaching is not a popularity contest. Not all students will like you. Not all students will appreciate your sense of humor. Not all students will learn from you. Even so, you must develop a certain thickness to your skin by shrugging it off and doing better next time with the next group. All teachers have a bad class sometime; all have one or two students that seem to ruin the rest of the class. Fight it off—try not to yield to the perceptions of a few; instead approach each day with renewed energy and commitment to do the best you can.

In this section, we discuss the entire teaching evaluation process in some detail. We hope you find teaching a rewarding and valuable experience. Teaching evaluations are the best and only way you can discover what you should or should not be doing. Teaching evaluations, in the final analysis, are the best and only way of becoming the kind of teacher you want to be. After all, teaching evaluations are a form of feedback—a way of discerning if students are receiving the message you intend.

Formal Student Feedback

Most universities, colleges, and departments require you to have students rate your teaching performance. Chairs and personnel committees often use such ratings as the primary source of information about your teaching effectiveness. You may also want to elicit summative or final course feedback to help plan for future course development and teaching strategies.

Research indicates that students seem to learn more with instructors they rate high in clarity of presentation, organization, and planning. Students who perceive themselves as having learned also tend to learn more. Of course, academic learning is not the only important criterion for assessing teaching effectiveness. You may want also your students to enjoy their college experience, be absent less often, develop positive self-concepts, and feel confidence in being able to prepare and deliver a speech. You may also want them to take more speech courses or choose a career in speech. Information obtained from student questionnaires can be a great help in reaching these goals. Results may also provide ideas about how to make changes in course content.

When you receive teaching evaluations, take the time to interpret exactly what the numbers mean. Use your evaluations as a form of feedback to help you improve—and to know what you're already doing right! What follows are some guidelines to help you accurately interpret your students' evaluations of your instruction:

- Compare your overall mean score with those obtained across all teachers in your department and college. Most departments provide that information. Examine individual item means, as well as the overall mean, to determine areas you need to work on. Importantly, you should emphasize also those areas that students really appreciated. Sometimes teachers forget to examine and reflect upon what students like.

- Consider the standard deviation from the mean for the department and school. This standard deviation tells you the range of differences around the mean. You should see if your mean falls into this range.

  Let's consider a hypothetical example. Let's say your mean score on a 5-point scale for the item "Rate the overall effectiveness of this teacher" is 4.2. Let's say the overall mean for the department for that item is 4.5. Is the difference between 4.2 and 4.5 (.3) meaningful—is it significant enough to warrant some concern from your chair or director? The standard deviation becomes critical here. If the standard deviation is greater than .3 (and it probably will be), then you don't have to worry. If the standard deviation is smaller, then you should feel compelled to work harder to increase your rating.

- Written feedback: Read all of your written comments, but don't let a single isolated negative comment embedded within a lot of other positive feedback trigger a backlash. Keep isolated comments in perspective. Once again, not everyone is going to like you (even if they should!). If others validate those negative perceptions, of course, you must treat them as legitimate, honest, and worth your scrutiny.

Informal Student Feedback

During the course, you may want to elicit informal feedback from your students as well. Why wait till the end of the term to determine what you did wrong (or right)? For example, you may ask them once a week or every three weeks to write down on a piece of paper some constructive feedback about how the course is going and your own teaching. The critical point of collecting this feedback is to *use* the feedback. That is, show your students that you are concerned about their learning experience. For example, if your students complain that they need extra time with you, you may want to consider changing your office hours, or you may need to come in early or stay late after class to accommodate them. The key is to respond to the feedback you receive from your students and to tell them when you do.

Guidelines to Help You Improve Your Teacher Ratings

Finally, here are a few suggestions to help you improve your teacher ratings and your overall teaching effectiveness:

1. Obtain a copy of the teacher evaluation form used by your department and examine each item carefully. Think of them as criteria for teaching effectiveness. Read them over again before you enter the classroom—each and every day. This procedure will help you keep in mind the important and relevant criteria on which students will be judging your teaching effectiveness. In this way, you will be in a better position to try to match your own teaching performance with the criteria your department has determined as important.

2. Organize your lessons carefully. You may want to put your outline on an overhead or on the board. (Transparency masters are available in Part 7.) Students will quickly get the idea that you are, in fact, organized. At the same time, you will have available your notes for teaching.

3. Strive for clarity in your explanations by using concrete examples and illustrations. Try to think of examples and stories *before* class. Sometimes applying the principles and concepts is harder than defining them. Immediately after giving your own illustration, ask your students to supply one or two more. In this way, they become actively involved in the learning experience—and you can see if they truly understand the concept.

4. Communicate enthusiasm for your subject and students. *Look* like you are excited to see them. Tell them so. No matter how tired you really are, no matter how depressed you may be, you are still obligated to give students your best in your role as an instructor. No students look forward to entering a classroom when they can predict that the teacher will be unpleasant, boring, and apathetic. Show them instead that you are committed to teaching, excited about the material, and anxious to be with them. Learn their names and use those names frequently in class. Make them feel special.

5. Keep all students involved. Try to elicit comments from everyone. Let them know that no matter what they say, their comments will be treated with respect. By example, show them that they can feel safe communicating with you and in front of their peers in your class.

6. Balance cognitive and affective goals. In other words, make sure that they learn the content, but at the same time try to get them to enjoy the material and the learning process. College experience should be exciting, challenging, and rewarding for students—help them believe that it is all of that and more.

7. Constantly broaden your knowledge in your area. Read the latest books; subscribe to and read the journals in communication. We can't impress upon you enough the importance of staying current in the field. Information changes so fast; what we thought was true yesterday may not be today. But more importantly, we are always learning new and interesting things about human communication behavior. There is so much to learn. There is so much we should know.

PART 7

TRANSPARENCY MASTERS

What follows are a series of outlines that can be easily transferred to transparencies for use with an overhead projector. Teachers who use these outlines report that students can more easily follow the lecture and discussion. With the use of transparencies, students discover what the teacher perceives as important and relevant information. As a result, students are more likely to take notes and study this information.

After course-testing this textbook across 50 or more teaching assistants and full-time faculty, we became highly selective in our efforts to choose just the right material to cover on each transparency. We hope you find each of these outlines useful for your own lectures and class discussion. More importantly, we hope your students find these transparencies useful for their learning.

When using the overhead projector, keep in mind all the rules involved in using visual aids for speeches. For instance, lecture with overheads sparingly; too many seem to distract students from paying attention to what you say. And make sure that you continue to face students when you use the overhead projector; look at them, not at the chart. Rely on a pointer to help students focus on key points and try covering up information on the chart that you are not yet ready to discuss.

1 A Communication-Based Model of Public Speaking

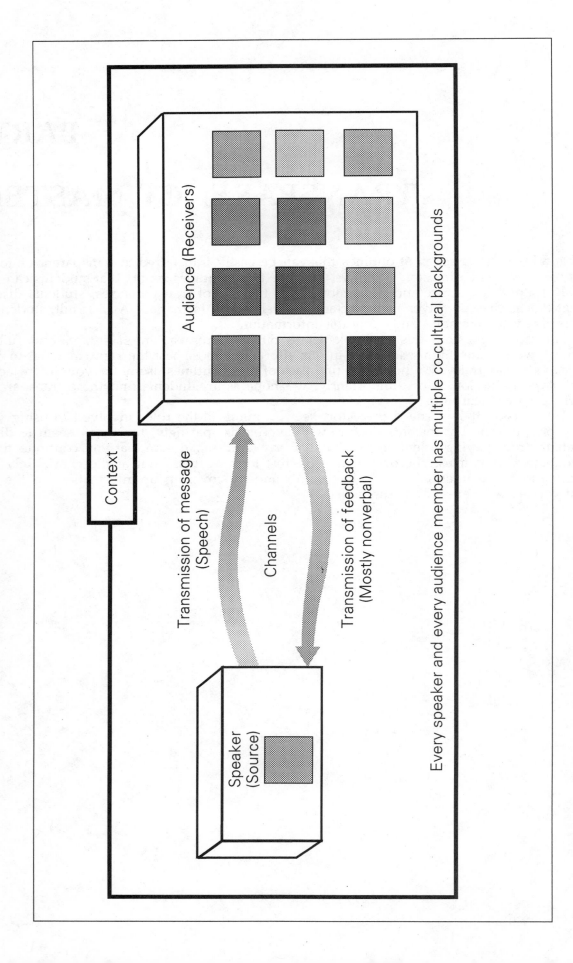

Kearney/Plax, *Public Speaking in a Diverse Society.* © 1996 Mayfield Publishing Company

Chapter 1, Fig. 1.2

Communication as Transaction

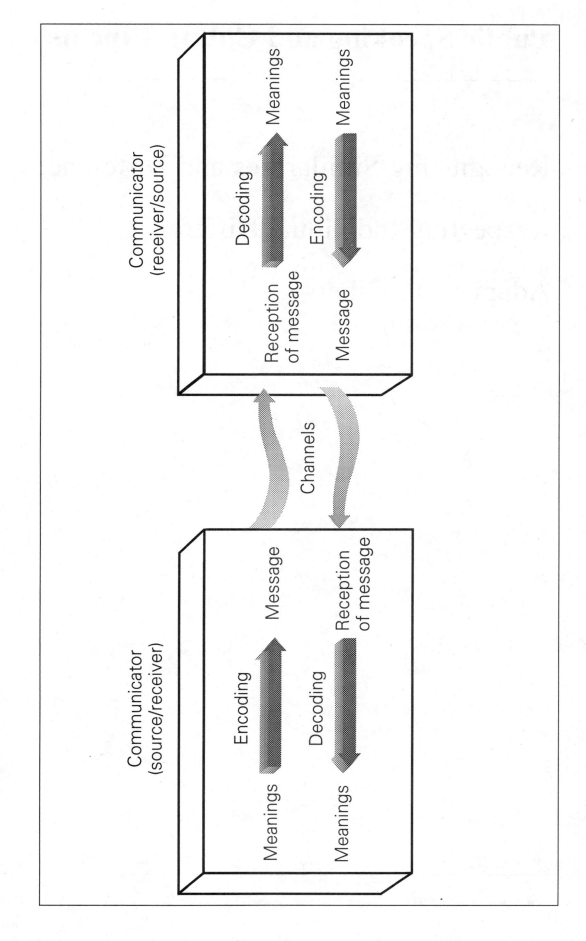

Kearney/Plax, Public Speaking in a Diverse Society. © 1996 Mayfield Publishing Company

3 Public Speaking and Cultural Inclusion

Recognizing Similarities and Differences

Respecting Individual Differences

Adapting to Others

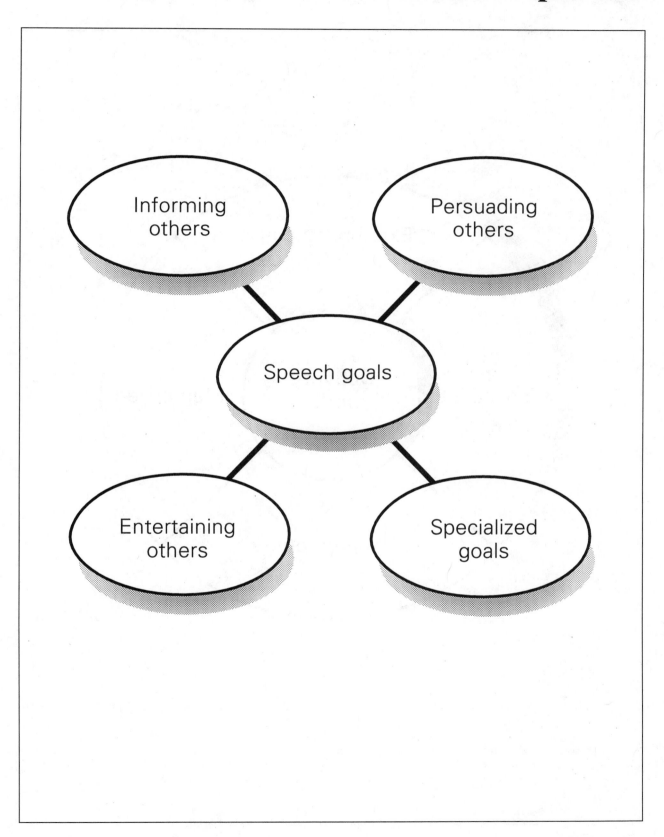

5   Modes of Speech Delivery

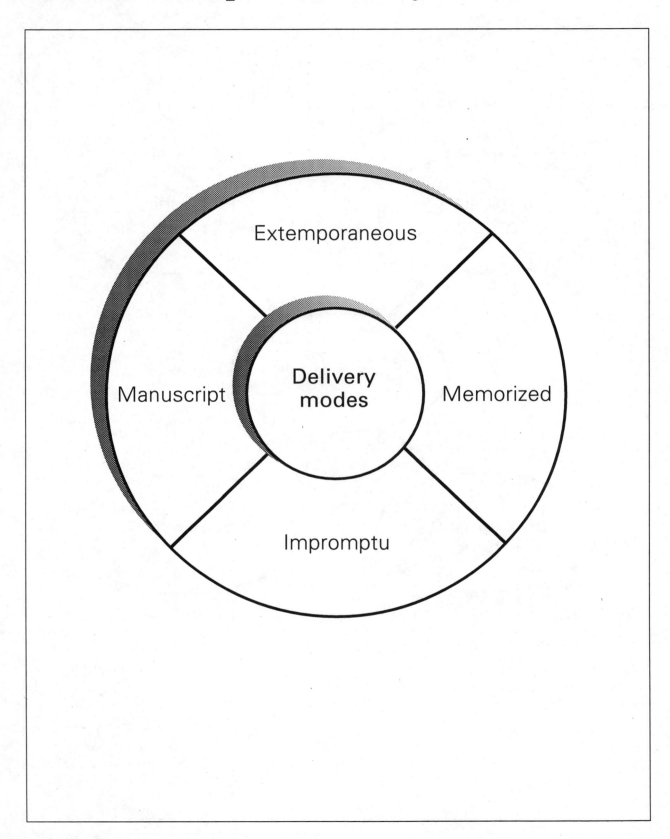

6 Steps in Preparing Your First Presentation

Analyze Your Audience

Select Your Topic

Research Your Subject

Organize and Outline Your Presentation

Rehearse Your Speech

7 Cultural Features That Make a Difference

Individualism and Collectivism

High and Low Context

High and Low Power, Rank, and Status

Masculinity and Femininity

8 Co-Culturally Unique Styles of Speaking

Euroamericans

African Americans

Latinos and Latinas

Asian Americans

Native Americans

Middle Eastern Americans

Females and Males

9 Possible Factors in Public Speaking Anxiety

Feeling conspicuous and inspected

Facing an unfamiliar or dissimilar audience

Confronting a novel or formal speaking situation

Undergoing evaluation

Feeling subordinate to your audience

Remembering repeated failures

Relying on English as a second language

10   Strategies for Managing Stage Fright

Select a familiar topic

Focus on the audience

Overprepare

Visualize a positive experience

Reduce fears through systematic desensitization, cognitive restructuring, or skills training

11   The Five Dimensions of Speaker Credibility

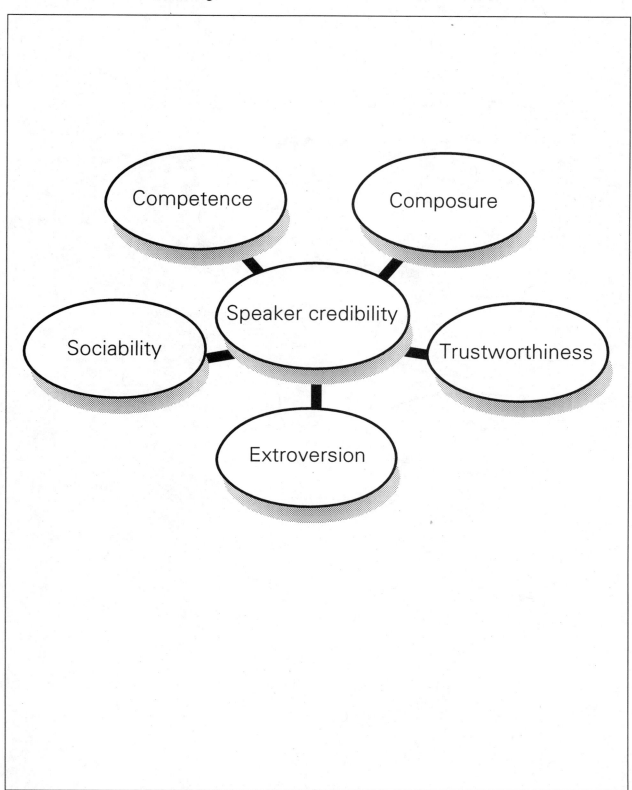

12 Ethical Obligations of Public Speakers

Present Evidence Truthfully

Reveal Sources Responsibly

Distinguish between Opinion and Fact

Respond to Questions Frankly

Respect Diversity of Argument and Opinion

Carefully Consider the Probable Effect of the Speech

Use Sound Reasoning in Persuasive Speaking

Be Responsible Using Appeals to Emotion and Values

13   Analyzing Your Audience

Audience Demographics

Audience Psychographics

Formal Methods of Analyzing Your Audience
- Focus group interviews
- Questionnaires or surveys

Creating a Profile of Your Audience

14   Adapting to Your Audience

Co-Culturally Dissimilar Audiences

Challenging Individuals and Situations
- Hostile audiences
- Hecklers
- Questioners
- Interjectors

15 Common Obstructions to Effective Listening

Inaccurate Assumptions about Listening
- "Listening is easy."
- "It's just a matter of intelligence."
- "Listening requires no planning."
- "If you know how to read, you know how to listen."

Five Barriers to Effective Listening
- Physical conditions
- Personal problems
- Co-cultural differences
- Co-cultural prejudices
- Connotative meanings

16   Selecting a Topic

Getting Started
- Determine the occasion
- Specify time constraints
- Identify your audience

Select a General Area or Subject
- Consider yourself
- Consider your audience
- Consider current events
- Boring topics or boring speakers?

Narrow the Topic

Specify Your Purpose

Formulate a Thesis Statement

17 Researching Your Topic

Types of Support

Gathering Information about Your Topic
- Rely on your own personal knowledge and experience
- Ask the experts directly
- Make use of the library

Select Only the Best Supporting Materials
- Is it relevant?
- Is it recent?
- Is it credible?

18 Using Linear Patterns to Organize Your Speech

Topical

Cause and Effect

Problem-Solution

Chronological

Spatial

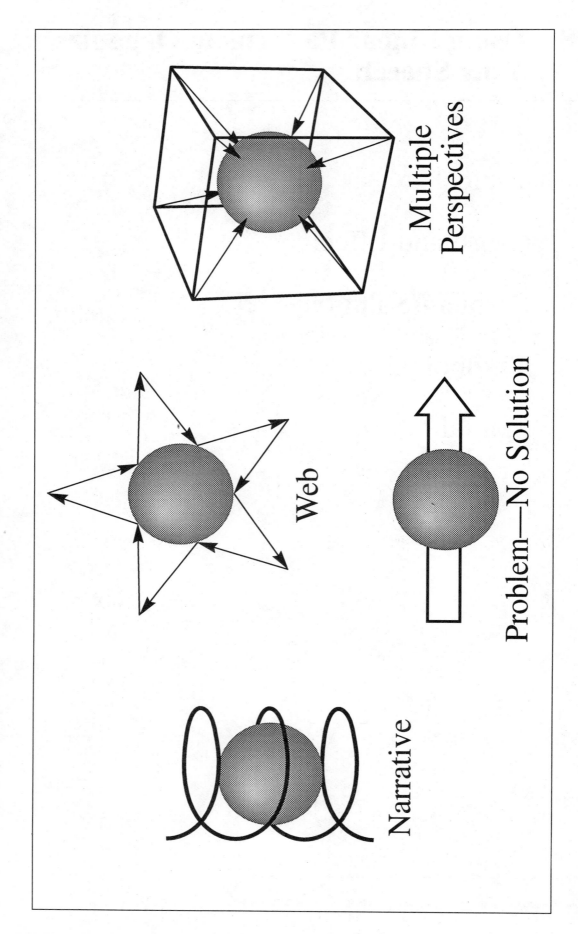

20 The Introduction: Beginning Your Speech

Establish Your Credibility

Compel Your Audience to Listen

Preview Your Speech

21 The Conclusion: Ending Your Speech

Summarize Your Speech

Leave Them Wanting More

22   Strategies to Grab and Motivate Your Audience

Personal Stories

Emotional Appeals

Humor

Repetition

Famous Quotations

Startling Facts and Statistics

Dramatic Illustrations

23 Goals of Informative Speaking

Communicating New and Unfamiliar
Information

Extending What the Audience Already
Knows

Updating Old Information

24 Four Basic Types of Informative Speeches

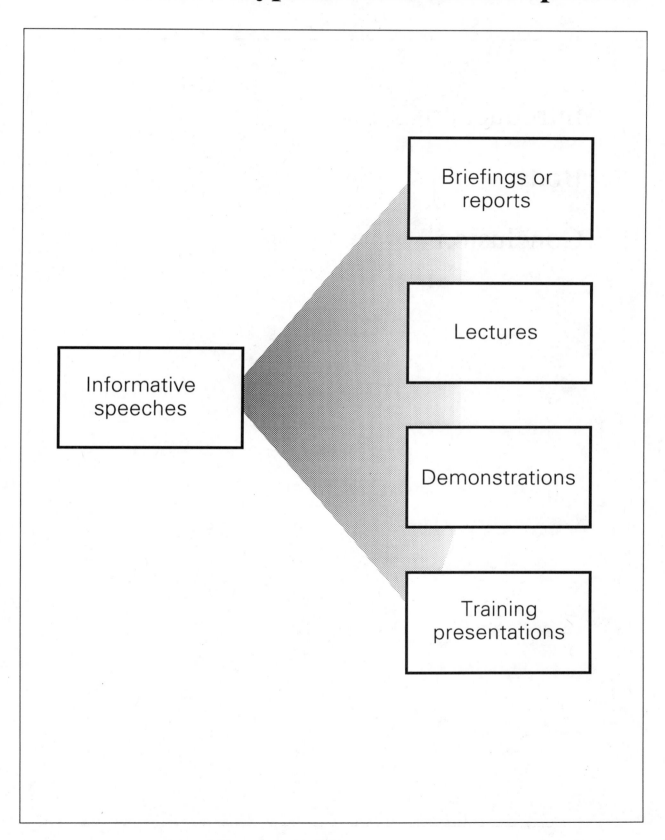

25 Organizing an Informative Speech

Introduction

Body

Conclusion

26 Strategies for Increasing Informational Effectiveness

Keep It Simple

Keep It Concrete

Be Repetitive and Redundant

Elicit Active Responses

Use Familiar and Relevant Examples

Use Transitions and Signposts

27 Goals of Persuasive Speaking

Changing Attitudes

Changing Beliefs

Changing Behavior

28 Five Basic Types of Persuasive Speeches

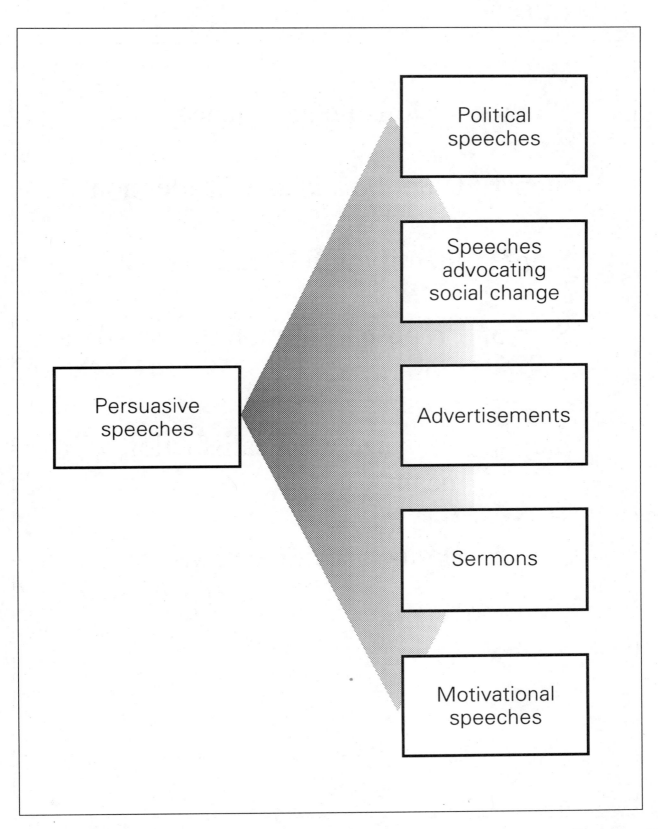

29 Organizing and Outlining a Persuasive Speech

Monroe's Motivated Sequence:

Step 1. Gain the audience's attention

Step 2. Identify unfulfilled needs

Step 3. Propose a solution that satisfies those needs

Step 4. Visualize what satisfaction will mean

Step 5. Define specific actions

30 Nine Strategies for Persuading

Conceal the Intent to Persuade

Don't Ask for Too Much

Avoid Inflammatory Phrases

Use a Two-Sided Message with Refutation

Inoculate against Counterarguments

Keep Objections to a Minimum

Combine Reason with Emotion

Use Fear Appeals — When Appropriate

Repeat Your Message

31 Verbal Communication: Making Every Word Count 1

Speak to Be Understood
- Keep it simple
- Limit your use of jargon and acronyms
- Avoid phrases that don't say anything
- Pronounce your words accurately
- Adapt to audience responses to your accent or dialect
- Appreciate your efforts to speak English as a second language

32 Verbal Communication: Making Every Word Count 2

Speak to Show Strength
- Use imaginative imagery

    Concrete images

    Similes

    Metaphors
- Use intense, animated language
- Choose the active voice
- Use power words and avoid unnecessary qualifiers

Speak to Include, Not Alienate
- Use bias-free language
    - Apply the principle of self-definition
    - Don't mention group membership unnecessarily
    - Give parallel treatment
    - Be inclusive and avoid making unwarranted assumptions
    - Don't use masculine terms as generics
    - Don't use feminine endings
    - Remember that people are people first
    - Watch for hidden bias
- Practice being verbally immediate
- Avoid profanity

34 Nonverbal Communication: Making Every Gesture Count

Look Like a Public Speaker
- Clothing communicates power and status
- Clothing communicates how we feel

Use Your Body Effectively
- Nonverbal emblems
- Nonverbal adaptors
- Nonverbal illustrators

Look at Your Audience

Keep Your Audience Interested

Use Your Voice to Your Advantage
- Vary vocal volume and pitch
- Vary speech rate
- Use silence strategically

Practice Being Nonverbally Immediate

35 Personal Communication Styles Well-Suited for Public Speaking

Dramatic Style

Animated Style

Open Style

Humorous Style

Feminine Communication Style

Masculine Communication Style

36 Guidelines for Effectively Using Visual Aids

Use Visual Aids That Serve a Definite Purpose

Use Visual Aids That Are Appropriate for Your Speech Topic, Your Audience, and the Occasion

Don't Overuse Visual Aids

Use Visual Aids That Require Little or No Explanation

Use Visual Aids That Catch and Hold Your Audience's Attention

Use Visual Aids That Are Easy to See

Keep Your Visual Aids in Your Possession during Your Presentation

Remove Your Visual Aids from Sight When You Are through with Them

Thoroughly Rehearse Using Your Visual Aids before Your Presentation

37 Public Speeches for Special Occasions

Ceremonial Speeches
- Introductions
- Welcomes
- Nominations
- Award speeches: Presenting and accepting
- Tributes: Eulogies and toasts
- Commencement speeches
- Dedications
- Farewells

38 Other Types of Specialized Public Presentations

Oral Performances of Literature

Entertaining Speeches

Question-and-Answer Sessions

Speaking in Groups
- Public discussions
- Symposiums
- Group forums
- Panel discussions

REFERENCES

Branan, J. M. (1972). Negative human interacting. *Journal of Counseling Psychology, 19,* 81–82.

Bloom, B. S., Engelhart, M. D., Furst, E. J., Hill, W. H., & Krathwohl, D. R. (1956). *Taxonomy of educational objectives handbook I: Cognitive domain.* New York: McKay.

Bloom, B. S., Hastings, J. T., & Madaus, G. F. (1971). *Handbook on formative and summarized evaluation of student learning.* New York: McGraw-Hill.

Bohn, C. A., & Bohn, E. (1985). Reliability of raters: The effects of rating errors on the speech rating process. *Communication Education, 34,* 343–351.

Check, J. F. (1979). Classroom discipline: Where are we now. *Education, 100,* 134–137.

Drayer, A. M. (1979). *Problems in middle and high school training: A handbook for student teachers and beginning teachers.* Boston, MA: Allyn & Bacon.

Good, T. L., & Brophy, J. E. (1987). *Looking in classrooms* (4th ed.). New York: Harper & Row.

Gronlund, N. (1982). *Constructing achievement tests* (3rd ed.). Englewood Cliffs, NJ: Prentice-Hall.

Harrow, A. J. (1972). *A taxonomy of psychomotor domain: A guide for developing behavioral objectives.* New York: McKay.

Hill, J. R. (1976). *Measurement and evaluation in the classroom.* Columbus: Charles E. Merrill.

Hurt, H. T., Scott, M. D., & McCroskey, J. C. (1978). *Communication in the classroom.* Readings, MA: Addison–Wesley.

Kaplan, R. (1974). Effects of learning with part vs. whole presentation of instructional objectives. *Journal of Educational Psychology, 66,* 787–792.

Kaplan, R., & Rothkopf, E. Z. (1974) Instructional objectives as directions to learners: Effects of passage length and amount of objective relevant content. *Journal of Educational Psychology, 66,* 448–456.

Kaplan, R., & Simmons, F. G. (1974). Effects of instructional objectives used as orienting stimuli or as summary/review upon prose learning. *Journal of Educational Psychology, 66,* 614–622.

Kearney, P., & McCroskey, J. C. (1980). Relationship among teacher communication style, trait, and state communication apprehension and teacher effectiveness. In D. Nimmo (ed.), *Communication yearbook 4* (pp. 533–552). New Brunswick, NJ: Transaction.

Kemp, J. E. (1985). *The instructional design process.* New York: Harper & Row.

Krathwohl, D. R., Bloom, B. S., & Masia, B. B. (1956). *Taxonomy of educational objectives handbook II: Affective domain.* New York: McKay.

Lashbrook, V. J., & Wheeless, L. R. (1978). Instructional communication theory and research: An overview of the relationship between learning theory and instructional communication. In B. D. Rubin (ed.), *Communication yearbook 2* (pp. 439–456). New Brunswick, NJ: Transaction.

Linn, R., Klein, S., & Hart, F. (1972). The nature and correlates of law school essay grades. *Educational and Psychological Measurement, 32,* 267–279.

McKeachie, W. J. (1986). *Teaching tips: A guidebook for the beginning college teacher* (8th ed.). Lexington, MA: D. C. Heath.

Mehrabian, A. (1971). *Silent messages.* Belmont, CA: Wadsworth.

Mouly, G. J. (1973). *Psychology for effective teaching.* New York: Holt, Rinehart & Winston.

Nash, P. P., Richmond, V. P., & Andriate, G. (1984). *Advanced instructional communication instructor's manual* (rev. ed.). Morgantown: West Virginia University Press.

Nungester, R. J., & Duchastel, P. C. (1982). Testing versus review: Effects on retention. *Journal of Educational Psychology, 74,* 18–22.

Popham, W., & Baker, E. (1970). *Establishing instructional goals.* Englewood Cliffs, NJ: Prentice-Hall.

Rothkopf, E. Z., & Kaplan, R. (1972). Exploration of the effect of density and specificity of instructional objectives on learning from text. *Journal of Psychology, 63,* 295–302.

Starch, D., & Elliott, E. C. (1912). Reliability of grading high school work in English, *School Review, 20,* 442–447.

Starch, D., & Elliott, E. C. (1913a). Reliability of grading work in history. *School Review, 12,* 676–681.

Starch, D., & Elliott, E. C. (1913b). Reliability of grading work in mathematics. *School Review, 21,* 676–681.

Woolfolk, A. E. & McCune-Nicolich, L. (1984). *Educational psychology for teachers* (2nd ed.). Englewood Cliffs, NJ: Prentice-Hall.